COUNTDOWN to CHRISTMAS

CHRISTMAS ON ITS WAY

BETTER HOMES AND GARDENS®

COUNTDOWN to CHRISTMAS

CHRISTMAS ON ITS WAY

CRAFTS EDITED BY KARIN STROM

RECIPES BY KATHY BLAKE

Better Homes and Gardens® Books

Des Moines, Iowa

Better Homes and Gardens®Books, an imprint of Meredith®Books:

President, Book Group: Joseph J. Ward
Vice President, Editorial Director: Elizabeth P. Rice
Executive Editor: Maryanne Bannon
Senior Editor: Carol Spier
Food Editor: Joyce Trollope
Associate Editor: Ruth Weadock

Countdown to Christmas: **CHRISTMAS ON ITS WAY**
was prepared and produced by
Michael Friedman Publishing Group, Inc.
15 West 26th Street
New York, New York 10010

Editor: Karla Olson
Production Editor: Loretta Mowat
Art Director: Jeff Batzli
Designer: Tanya Ross-Hughes
Photography Director: Christopher C. Bain
Illustrations: Roberta Frauwirth
Crafts Directions: Peggy Greig
Photography: Bill Milne

ISBN: 0-696-00047-4
Library of Congress Catalog Card Number: 93-080860

10 9 8 7 6 5 4 3 2 1

Printed and bound in China

Our seal assures you that every recipe in *Countdown to Christmas: CHRISTMAS ON ITS WAY* has been tested in the Better Homes and Gardens®Test Kitchen. This means that each recipe is practical and reliable, and meets our high standards of taste appeal. We guarantee your satisfaction with this book for as long as you own it.

All of us at Better Homes and Gardens®Books are dedicated to offering you, our customer, the best books we can create. We are particularly concerned that all of our instructions for making projects are clear and accurate. Please address your correspondence to Customer Service, Meredith®Press, 150 East 52nd Street, New York, NY 10022.

If you would like to order additional copies of any of our books, call 1-800-678-2803 or check with your local bookstore.

ACKNOWLEDGMENTS

Karin Strom would like to acknowledge the following people: Peggy Greig, Roberta Frauwirth, all the talented crafts people who contributed, Karla Olson for her perseverance, Carol Spier for her patience, Chris Bain for his moral support, The Inn at Mill Race Pond for use of their lovely site during photography, and, of course, Colin, Viola, and Nadine for being there during a year of Christmas.

Kathy Blake would like to acknowledge the following people: Amelia Franklin, Gail Berry, and Laurie Middleton for help with testing and tasting, and Joyce Trollope and the Better Homes and Gardens® Test Kitchen for more testing and tasting.

Contents

INTRODUCTION

If you're someone who loves to create a personal Christmas each year, baking delectable treats for guests and crafting delightful gifts and decorations by hand, you know that Christmas can be a hectic climax of celebration and gift-giving. In **Better Homes and Gardens**® *Countdown to Christmas* series, you'll find a step-by-step guide to the easiest and most memorable holiday season ever.

The secret is getting a head start, and keeping organized along the way. Beginning with *Countdown to Christmas: Christmas On Its Way*, filled with fantastic storable recipes and beautiful handmade gifts and decorations to craft, you'll prepare early—by making jams, jellies, spice mixes, and more, using fresh, seasonal ingredients at their most flavorful. And, knowing that you have plenty of time before the holiday, you can make lots of exquisite gifts and accessories— each of heirloom quality, each a personal expression of appreciation and love.

As the holiday approaches, take advantage of the recipes and crafts projects in other *Countdown to Christmas* volumes. *Christmas 'Round the Corner* offers delicious recipes to freeze in anticipation of the holiday season, and charming, not-too-time-consuming gift ideas to craft ahead of time. *'Tis the Season* is filled with quick, last-minute gifts and decorating projects for the time when you're busiest. In it you'll find recipes for fabulous feasts and holiday entertaining, with menu suggestions that can (but don't have to) incorporate many of the foods you prepared from the pages of *Christmas On Its Way* and *Christmas 'Round the Corner*.

Better Homes and Gardens® *Countdown to Christmas* series is full of delicious Christmas recipes and great gift and decorating ideas. Each volume includes timely recipes and complete directions for crafts, and can be enjoyed on its own. Together, the books will really help you plan your holiday ahead and stay on track. If you wish, you can follow the suggestions for using foods you've prepared earlier or scraps left from your heirloom projects, but—even if you didn't have a chance to freeze your pie filling when the fruit was fresh or make the Pine Tree Quilt—you'll be able to complete any of the recipes or projects you wish.

There's no time like Christmas, with its warm well-wishing and gifts of love, enchanting decorations, and mouthwatering cuisine. There's plenty of time before Christmas for planning ahead—to make the most of the season as it arrives, so you can share in its joy and celebrate in style.

BEGIN COUNTING THE DAYS NOW!

Early autumn is not too soon for getting out the calendar and developing a "holiday attack plan." For the months of November and December, mark down all the events you already know will be occurring—the school pageant, when vacation starts, affairs you attend annually. Then mark in target dates for when you want to complete craft projects, send out the Christmas cards, begin Christmas baking, start decorating the house. While some of these dates can't be set in stone, you will get a realistic picture of what will need to be done and when. Having things down on paper can help alleviate the feeling of panic that sometimes sets in as Christmas approaches. Get started early and you'll enjoy the holidays more.

CHRISTMAS CRAFTS

PART

1

It's
midsummer.
The flowers are
blooming, the children
are home from school, and
you're thinking about Christmas!
"Why?" some of your friends are wondering,
"Why Christmas in July?" You know that there
are plenty of reasons to begin holiday preparations
as early as possible. The pace is slower during the summer
months, giving you more time to plan what you want to give
to whom. Thinking ahead means there's time to do more ambitious
crafts projects and have them finished before the busy holiday season
begins. Loved ones enjoy receiving (and using, displaying, and eating)
gifts made especially
for them, and adding
pieces to your family's
heirloom collection is
a lasting pleasure. Let
the holidays begin!

All Through the House

BEFORE YOU FOCUS ON GIFTS
FOR EVERYONE ELSE, WHY NOT
PLAN A WONDERFUL TREAT TO
MAKE FOR YOUR OWN HOME?
THIS IS THE PERFECT TIME TO
START SOMETHING THAT WILL
BECOME A FAMILY HEIRLOOM.

HOME AND HEARTS SAMPLER

Everyone agrees that the heart of the holidays is at home. This enchanting cross-stitch sampler expresses that sentiment perfectly, combining charmingly naive elements from traditional samplers. Evergreen trees, snowflakes, and a welcoming wreath on the front door of the house add Christmas cheer. These motifs can be translated to other needlework projects, such as ornaments, sachets, or pillows. Whether you make this sampler to give as a gift or to keep as an addition to your own decor, it is certain to become a holiday heirloom.

SIZE

- Sampler is 11" x 14".

YOU WILL NEED

- Six-strand embroidery floss: 3 skeins each cranberry, forest green, slate blue; 1 skein each dark gray, light gray, tan, dark cranberry, sea green, mustard, rust, straw, off-white, and brown
- 17" x 20" piece 14-count Aida cloth in off-white
- Embroidery hoop and needle
- Frame (optional)*

DIRECTIONS

CROSS-STITCHING: Finish edges of cloth to prevent raveling. With contrasting thread, baste horizontal and vertical centers of fabric. Center design on fabric, matching fabric center with center of chart. Following chart and key, work cross-stitch with three strands of floss (see above right). Work backstitch with two strands of floss. When embroidery is finished, hand wash fabric in cold water. Dry flat and press on a well-padded

HOW TO CROSS-STITCH

Use an evenweave fabric. To prevent raveling, zigzag or whipstitch raw edges. Place fabric in an embroidery hoop to keep taut while stitching. To avoid creases, do not leave work in hoop when not stitching. Cut floss into 18" lengths; separate to number of strands specified. Use an embroidery or tapestry needle. Do not knot your thread.

Each cross-stitch is made over the intersection of one lengthwise and one crosswise thread on the fabric. Always pass the needle through the "holes," not the threads. Begin by bringing needle up through fabric, leaving a 1" strand of floss on back. Hold this strand in the direction you are stitching; secure by stitching over it.

The cross-stitch is made in two steps: You form an "X" by passing the floss diagonally across the fabric threads in two directions (A). Be sure all 1–2 stitches are underneath, and all 3–4 stitches are on top. When making a row of adjacent stitches in the same color, work the 1–2 stitches of the "X" the required number of times, then work back, "crossing" all the stitches with 3–4 top stitches (B). When making adjacent stitches, pass the needle through the same hole more than once. To secure end of floss, slide the needle under several stitches on the back of work and snip excess floss.

Each symbol on chart represents one cross-stitch; different symbols represent different colors. Do not carry floss across back from one color area to another.

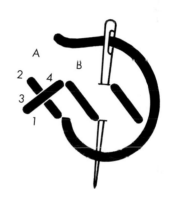

surface. Following manufacturer's instructions, mount and frame sampler.

*If you would like an heirloom quality cross-stitch project, we recommend taking the completed, pressed piece to a professional framer who has had experience framing needlework. You've already invested your time—it's worth protecting that investment!

EMBROIDERY FLOSS: *Anchor*

■ *Home and Hearts Sampler Chart*

HOLIDAY CROSS-STITCH

Cross-stitch makes a perfect traveling companion. Take projects along on summer vacation trips. No matter how you go—by car, train, or plane—an extra tote bag with a needlework project-in-progress provides a welcome break from travel tedium. Store embroidery floss in small self-sealing plastic bags and the fabric you are stitching in a larger one to protect it from beach sand, moisture, and other hazards of summer.

CENTER

CENTER

CENTER

COLOR KEY

DMC		ANCHOR	
816	☒	20	cranberry
699	◣	423	forest green
930	◩	922	slate blue
413	⊟	401	dark gray
318	▯	399	light gray
640	T	903	tan
902	◼	72	dark cranberry
320	6	215	sea green
832	⌐	907	mustard
919	V	340	rust
926	⤢	850	straw
746	•	275	off-white
838	Z	380	brown
—			Back stitch with light gray

PINE TREE QUILT

Hanging on a wall, covering a bed, or draped over a sofa, this handsome patchwork quilt brings Christmas cheer to almost any room of the house during the holidays and after. While the colors in the tiny print fabrics and the evergreen tree motif do suggest Christmas, the simplicity of the design makes it a striking piece to display all year long.

The tree blocks are machine stitched and pieced and the quilting is worked by hand with metallic gold thread for a subtle glistening effect. Consider making extra tree blocks to use for matching pillows.

ENLARGING PATTERNS

With ruler and pencil, extend the grid lines over the diagram. On paper, draw a grid of squares in the size indicated by the scale given with the diagram, being sure your grid has the same number of rows and columns of squares as the original. Refer to the diagram and mark the full-size grid where the pattern lines intersect with the grid lines. Connect the markings. Refine any details if necessary.

SIZE

- Quilt is 62" x 78".

YOU WILL NEED

- Cotton print fabrics: 1 yd each assorted creams and greens; 1/4 yd assorted browns; 1 1/2 yds cream for alternate blocks; 2 yds red for border; 5 yds 45" wide backing fabric
- Twin-size low-loft quilt batting
- 1 spool white thread
- 2 spools gold metallic thread
- 3 pkgs brown double fold quilt binding
- Scissors, pencil, and cardboard
- Tracing paper for pattern
- Masking tape, 1 1/2" wide
- Quilting needle

DIRECTIONS

NOTE: Templates include 1/4" seam allowance.

PREPARE PIECES: Enlarge patterns (see left). Using tracing paper and pencil, trace patterns onto cardboard to use as templates. Cut out. Using templates and from assorted cream prints, cut 48 A triangles and 12 C pieces. Reverse C template and cut 12 mirror image C pieces from same fabrics. From assorted green prints, cut 12 A triangles and 36 B pieces. From assorted brown prints, cut 12 D pieces for tree trunks. From cream print, cut six squares, each 12 1/2", for solid blocks. Cut five squares, each 12 7/8"; cut each in half diagonally for ten setting triangles. Cut two squares, each 18 1/2"; cut each in half diagonally for four corner triangles. From red print, cut two side border strips, each 7" x 67 1/2", and top and bottom border strips, each 7" x 62". Cut backing fabric into two 2 1/2-yd pieces.

PIECING: Following piecing diagram on page 22, join long edge of green A piece to upper edge of green B to make tree top. Join a cream C to each short edge of a green B to make tree center. Join a cream A to each short edge of green B to make lower part of tree top. Join short edge of cream A to straight edge of brown D to make tree trunk. Join these four units to make a tree block. Make 12 blocks.

ASSEMBLY: Following assembly diagram, join tree blocks, cream squares, and side and corner triangles to form diagonal rows. Join rows to make quilt top. Join red side border strips to sides of quilt. Sew top and bottom borders to quilt and side edges of border strips. With right sides together and using 1/4" seam allowance, sew two pieces of backing fabric together lengthwise.

QUILTING: Lay backing fabric wrong side up on working surface. Center batting on backing, then place quilt top right side up on top. Beginning at center, baste layers together. With gold metallic thread, hand quilt 1/4" to inside of tree motif. With a length of masking tape, mark horizontal center of plain blocks. Hand quilt along edge of tape. Remove tape and then place edge along line just quilted and quilt another line parallel to first. Following assembly diagram, repeat lines of quilting across entire block, with quilting lines 1 1/2" apart on each square. Repeat on corner and side triangles. With tape, mark a zigzag with points 9" apart across width of border. Hand quilt along marked lines.

FINISHING: Trim backing and batting even with quilt top. Machine stitch binding to sides of quilt. Folding in cut ends, stitch binding to top and bottom of quilt. Fold binding to wrong side of quilt and slipstitch in place.

THREAD: Coats Dual Duty Plus white thread; Coats Gold Metallic thread **BINDING:** Coats Double Fold Quilt Binding

- *Pine Tree Quilt Piecing Diagram*

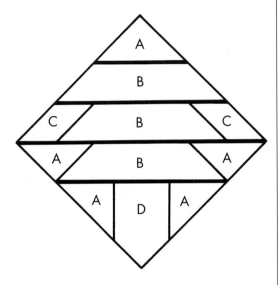

- *Pine Tree Quilt Assembly Diagram*

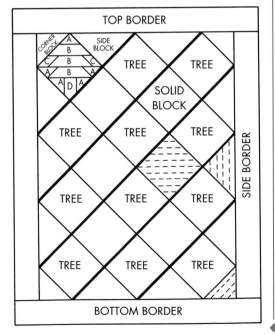

- - - - =quilting lines

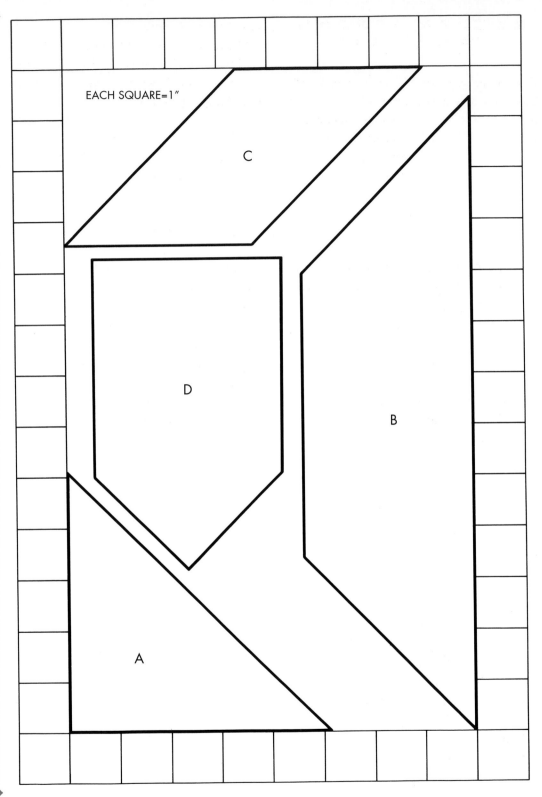

EACH SQUARE=1″

- *Pine Tree Quilt Pattern*

GOLDEN RIBBON PILLOWS

One clever way to transform a room for the holidays is to add a collection of festive throw pillows to the sofa, love seat, or side chairs. Opulent metallic ribbons combined with rich fabrics in interesting patterns create a luxurious effect. As shown, these elegant pillows complement almost any decor, or you can alter the tones to better suit your color scheme.

SIZES

- Tattersall pillow is 18" square. Diamond pillow is 16" square. Striped pillow is 14" square. Rectangular pillow is 12" x 16". Neck bolster is 6" x 14".

YOU WILL NEED

FOR EACH PILLOW:

- 1/2 yd white or off-white medium weight fabric such as linen or chintz
- 1/2 yd 3/4" wide Velcro® Sew-On hook and loop tape
- Basting glue stick
- Matching thread
- Scissors, pencil, and cardboard

FOR TATTERSALL PILLOW:

- 3 yds 7/8" wide gold and white polka-dotted ribbon
- 2 yds 1/2" wide white twisted cording
- 18" square pillow form

FOR DIAMOND PILLOW:

- 1 yd each 1 1/2" wide off-white and gold paisley ribbon and 3/4" wide sheer gold chevron ribbon
- 2 yds 1/4" wide off-white twisted cording
- 16" square pillow form

FOR STRIPED PILLOW:

- 1 1/2 yd each 1 1/2" wide gold-trimmed white ribbon and 1" wide diamond sheer ribbon
- 1 1/2 yd 1/4" wide white twisted cording
- 14" square pillow form

FOR RECTANGULAR PILLOW:

- 1 1/2 yd 3/4" wide greek key gold ribbon
- 1 1/2 yd 1/4" wide gold twisted cording
- 12" x 16" pillow form

FOR NECK BOLSTER:

- 2 yds 2 1/2" wide gold dot ribbon
- 1 yd 1/4" wide white twisted cording
- 6" x 14" pillow form

DIRECTIONS

NOTE: Pillow forms are usually slightly smaller than the measurement indicated. Measure the pillow form before cutting fabric to be certain that the finished pillowcase will fit the pillow form snugly.

TATTERSALL PILLOW: From white or off-white fabric, cut an 18" square. Cut ribbon into six pieces, each 18" long. Using glue stick and referring to photo, baste ribbons in place on pillow front in tattersall pattern. Sew in place. From white or off-white fabric, cut two rectangles, each 10" x 18". On one piece, press long edge 1/2" to wrong side. On wrong side, cover folded edge with hook side of Velcro® and sew in place. Press 1/2" to right side along long edge on second rectangle. Sew loop side of Velcro® over folded edge. Close pillow back along Velcro® and trim excess to make an 18" square. With right sides of pillow front and back together, sew around all four sides with a 1/2" seam allowance. Trim corners. Open Velcro® and turn pillow cover right side out. Whipstitch cording in place around outside edges. Insert pillow form.

DIAMOND PILLOW: From white or off-white fabric, cut a 16" square. Cut each ribbon into four pieces, each 16" long. Using glue stick and referring to photo, baste ribbons in place on pillow front, turning in ribbon ends to form a diamond pattern. Sew in place. From white or off-white fabric, cut two rectangles, each 9" x 16". On one piece, press long edge 1/2" to wrong side. On wrong side, cover folded edge

with hook side of Velcro® and sew in place. Press 1/2" to right side along long edge on second rectangle. Sew loop side of Velcro® over folded edge. Close pillow back along Velcro® and trim off excess to make a 16" square. With right sides of pillow front and back together, sew around all sides with a 1/2" seam allowance. Trim corners. Open Velcro® and turn pillow cover right side out. Whipstitch cording in place around outside edges. Insert pillow form.

STRIPED PILLOW: From white or off-white fabric, cut a 14" square. Cut ribbons into 14" lengths. Using glue stick and referring to photo, baste ribbons in place on pillow front in striped pattern, beginning and ending with narrow ribbon. Sew in place. From white or off-white fabric, cut two rectangles, each 8" x 14". On one piece, press long edge 1/2" to wrong side. On wrong side, cover folded edge with hook side of Velcro® and sew in place. Press 1/2" to right side along long edge on second rectangle. Sew loop side of Velcro® over folded edge. Close pillow back along Velcro® and trim off excess to make a 14" square. With right sides of front and back of pillow together, sew around all sides with a 1/2" seam allowance. Trim corners. Open Velcro® and turn pillow cover right side out. Whipstitch cording in place around outside edges. Insert pillow form.

RECTANGULAR PILLOW: From white or off-white fabric, cut a 12" x 16" rectangle. Cut ribbon into four lengths, two each 12" long and two each 16" long. Using glue stick and referring to photo, baste ribbons in place on pillow front in rectangle pattern. Sew in place. From white or off-white fabric, cut two rectangles, each 9" x 12". On one piece, press short edge 1/2" to wrong side. On wrong side,

cover folded edge with hook side of Velcro® and sew in place. Press 1/2" to right side along short edge on second rectangle. Sew loop side of Velcro® over folded edge. Close pillow back along Velcro® and trim off excess to make a 12" x 16" rectangle. With right sides of front and back of pillow together, sew around all sides with a 1/2" seam allowance. Trim corners. Open Velcro® and turn pillow cover right side out. Whipstitch cording in place around outside edges. Insert pillow form.

NECK BOLSTER: From white or off-white fabric, cut a 14" x 20" rectangle and cut two circles, each 7" in diameter. Cut ribbon into three lengths, each 20" long. Using glue stick and referring to photo, baste ribbons in place on rectangle in striped pattern. Sew in place. Press 1/2" to wrong side on one short edge of rectangle. Cover folded edge with hook side

of Velcro® and sew in place. Press 1/2" over to right side along opposite short edge. Sew loop side of Velcro® over folded edge. Turn to wrong side and close pillow along Velcro® edges. With right sides together, pin circles to long edges, easing to fit. Sew in place. Clip along seam every 1/2". Open Velcro® and turn pillow cover right side out. Whipstitch cording in place around pillow ends. Insert pillow form.

RIBBONS: C.M. Offray and Son

SNOWFLAKE AFGHAN

Are you already dreaming of a white Christmas? On a cold, snowy night, what could be better than to wrap yourself or a loved one in this lovely snowflake afghan? Metallic silver threads worked in with the snow white floss add a shimmering glow to a rich blue ground. The snowflake motifs may be used as a border design, as shown here, or stitched on every block of the Honeybee cloth, in an allover pattern.

SIZE

- Afghan is 45" x 58".

YOU WILL NEED

- 1 1/4 yds Zweigart Honeybee 14-count fabric in Victorian Blue #510
- 15 skeins white embroidery floss
- 8 spools silver metallic blending filament
- Embroidery hoop and size 24 tapestry needle

DIRECTIONS

CROSS-STITCHING: Design is worked over two threads in a 49-stitch square that is pre-woven in fabric. With contrasting basting thread, baste horizontal and vertical centers of each square along the outer edges of fabric. Center cross-stitch design in square, matching square center with center of chart. Following chart and key (see page 17), work cross-stitch with three strands of floss and two strands of blending filament held together. Follow manufacturer's instructions for working with blending filament as it frays easily. When embroidery is finished, hand wash fabric in cold water. Dry flat and press on a well-padded surface.

FINISHING: Machine zigzag 1" from fabric edges. Fringe beyond stitching.

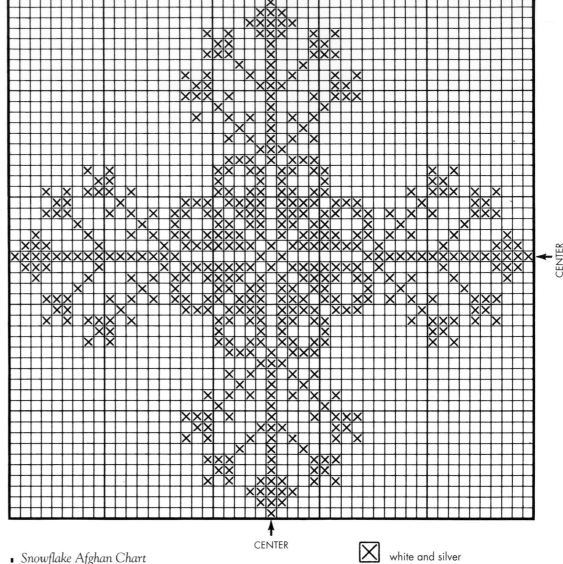

CENTER

- *Snowflake Afghan Chart*

☒ white and silver

EMBROIDERY FLOSS: DMC **METALLIC BLENDING FILAMENT:** *Kreinik*

Deck the Halls

WE LOVE TO HAVE FABULOUS THINGS SURROUNDING US AT CHRISTMAS—HANDMADE STOCKINGS, UNIQUE TREE ORNAMENTS, ONE-OF-A-KIND CHRISTMAS TREE SKIRTS. SET SOME TIME ASIDE THIS SUMMER TO MAKE A FEW SPECIAL OBJECTS TO ADD TO YOUR COLLECTION OF DECORATIONS OR TO GIVE AS GIFTS.

Opulent Ornaments

Glistening from the branches, spinning on the boughs, Christmas tree ornaments capture the magic of Christmas. Our collection of ornaments includes intricately beaded and be-ribboned Victorian Shapes, Ribbon Embroidered Geometrics stitched on plastic canvas, and fragrant jewel-tone Potpourri Ornaments. Placed on the tree or displayed on the mantel or tabletop, these tiny treasures prove that "good things come in small packages."

TRIMMING THE TREE

There are two schools of thought when it comes to tree trimming. With the theme tree approach, the tree is decorated in a consistent theme or color scheme. On the eclectic tree, a diverse collection of ornaments, gathered over the years, is displayed with panache. Whichever approach is more your style, one rule applies: One can never have too many ornaments. Indeed, it's hard to resist adding a few special decorations to one's collection each year. Ornaments are lightweight, easy to store, and relatively inexpensive, and can be gloriously displayed in many different ways. An ornament, purchased or handcrafted, also makes a perfect hostess gift or holiday party favor.

VICTORIAN SHAPES

SIZES

- Each ornament is approximately 4".

YOU WILL NEED

FOR EACH ORNAMENT:
- 12" square piece of moiré fabric in pink, blue, or mint
- ½ yd narrow lace
- 1 skein white rayon embroidery floss
- 1 pkg each sew-on pearls: 2½mm, 3 mm, and 3x6mm (1 pkg will make several ornaments)
- ½ yd each ⅛" wide white satin ribbon and ³⁄₁₆" wide white satin picot ribbon
- ½ yd tiny string pearls
- Polyester stuffing
- Embroidery hoop and needle
- Dressmaker's carbon
- Hot glue gun and glue sticks or thick white craft glue
- Thread to match fabrics
- White thread
- Scissors

DIRECTIONS

EMBROIDERY: Trace two actual size patterns for each ornament onto moiré using dressmaker's carbon. Do not cut. Place one piece of fabric in embroidery hoop and following chart for stitches, with six strands of floss, embroider designs on one piece for front. Sew pearls in place with white thread. Cut out ornament front and back, adding ¼" seam allowance. Hand baste lace to ornament front, matching raw edges. Cut a 3" length of picot ribbon and fold in half. Pin to top of ornament for hanging loop.

ASSEMBLY: With right sides together, sew front and back of ornament together, leaving small opening for turning. Trim curves and turn. Press lightly. Stuff and slipstitch opening closed. Referring to photo, tie ribbon into bows and glue to ornament. Tie string pearls into bow and glue in place onto ribbon bow. Make tiny bow from picot ribbon and glue in place at front of cone ornament.

LACE: *Wrights Trims* RIBBONS: *C.M. Offray and Son* FLOSS: *Anchor Marlitt*

FRENCH KNOTS

STEP 1: Bring needle up through fabric where knot is to be made (1). Wind thread around point of needle two or three times.

STEP 2: Insert needle into fabric close to spot where needle emerged (2). Pull to wrong side, holding stitch in place.

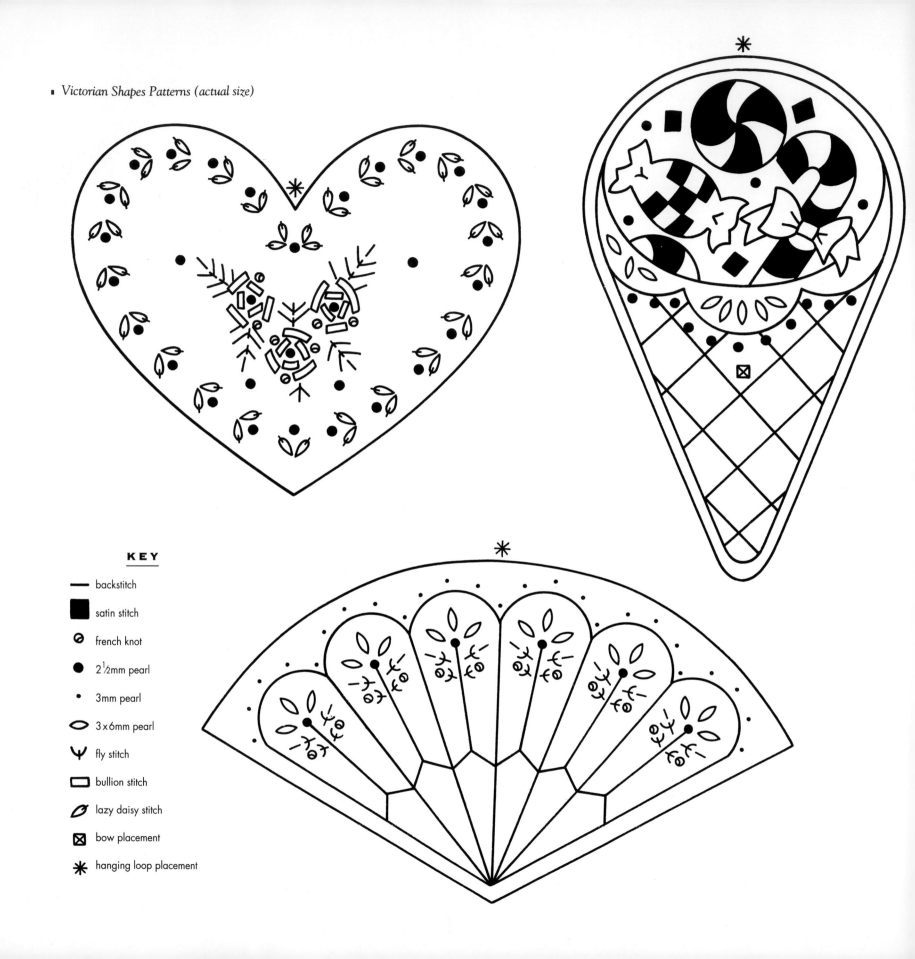

▪ *Victorian Shapes Patterns (actual size)*

KEY

——	backstitch
■	satin stitch
⊘	french knot
●	2½mm pearl
•	3mm pearl
⬯	3 x 6mm pearl
Ψ	fly stitch
▭	bullion stitch
⬭	lazy daisy stitch
⊠	bow placement
✳	hanging loop placement

RIBBON EMBROIDERED GEOMETRICS

SIZES

- Each ornament is approximately 4".

YOU WILL NEED

FOR EACH ORNAMENT:

- 4" square 10-count plastic canvas
- Large tapestry needle
- Scissors
- Hot glue gun and glue sticks

FOR MINT DIAMOND:

- 13 yds ⅛" wide mint satin ribbon (MC); 7 yds white (CC); 1 yd ⅜" wide picot-edged white satin ribbon

FOR PURPLE DIAMOND:

- 12 yds ⅛" wide purple satin ribbon (MC); 6 yds red (CC); ½ yd ⅝" wide gold metallic ribbon
- 4 red 8mm faceted beads
- 3 purple 6mm faceted beads
- 11 gold craft beads
- Purple thread

FOR EMERALD DROP:

- 8 yds ⅛" wide emerald satin ribbon (MC); 4 yds royal blue (CC); ½ yd ⅝"

wide gold metallic ribbon

- 6 green 8mm beads
- 3 blue 8mm beads
- 12 gold craft beads
- Emerald thread

FOR ROSE DROP:

- 9 yds ⅛" wide rose satin ribbon (MC); 4 yds white (CC); 1 yd ⅜" wide picot-edged white satin ribbon

FOR BLUE RECTANGLE:

- 9 yds ⅛" wide capri satin ribbon (MC); 6 yds white (CC); 1 yd ⅜" wide picot-edged white satin ribbon

FOR RED RECTANGLE:

- 8 yds ⅛" wide red satin ribbon (MC); 5 yds emerald (CC); ½ yd ⅝" wide gold metallic ribbon
- 3 green 8mm beads
- 1 red 8mm bead
- 7 gold craft beads
- Red thread

DIRECTIONS

STITCHING: See "Working Canvas," page 34. Cover the canvas with diagonal stitches as indicated on the charts. Keep ribbon smooth with no twists, and take care not to pierce ribbon with needle as you work. To secure beginning ribbon end, lay cut end flat against plastic canvas and work several stitches over it. Following appropriate chart, stitch plastic canvas. End each ribbon length by threading under stitches already worked. Cut out shape when stitching is complete. Cut along inside edges of Diamonds. To finish the edges of canvas, overcast exposed bar, stitching in alternate squares, all the way around the ornament. Reversing stitch direction, work ribbon in empty squares, creating a braided effect.

FINISHING: PASTEL GROUP: Cut a 6" length of picot ribbon and fold in half. Glue to top of ornament with hot glue gun for hanging loop. Tie a bow with picot and narrow ribbons held together and glue to loop. Trim ribbon ends.

BRIGHT GROUP: Form loops and bows with gold ribbons as for Pastel group. String needle with matching thread doubled and stitch loops and bows to ornament. Following photo for placement, string beads onto thread and position on ornament. Finish with gold bead, then pull needle back through beads to secure. Secure thread end to ornament with tiny stitches.

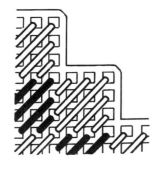

WORKING CANVAS

Each symbol on the charts represents one stitch and indicates the number of mesh to cover and the direction in which to work. When stitching is complete, cut the canvas between the bars *outside* the last row of stitches, leaving a bar exposed. Trim any nubs.

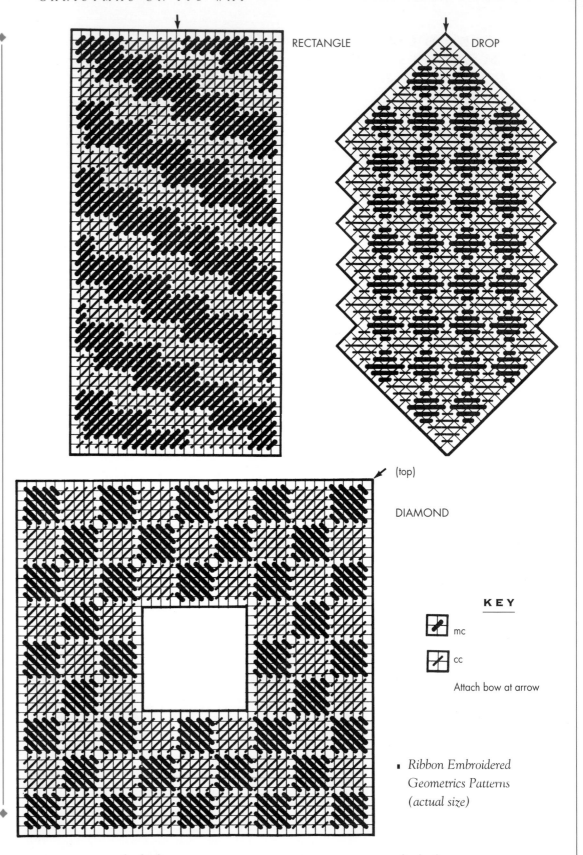

RECTANGLE

DROP

(top)

DIAMOND

KEY

mc

cc

Attach bow at arrow

Ribbon Embroidered Geometrics Patterns (actual size)

POTPOURRI ORNAMENTS

SIZES

- Each ornament is approximately 4".

YOU WILL NEED

FOR EACH ORNAMENT:

- 6" x 8" piece paper-backed fusible web
- 6" x 8" piece silk or lamé fabric
- 6" x 8" piece matching or contrasting backing fabric
- 6" square gold dotted tulle
- 1 spool gold metallic thread
- 1 spool white thread
- 1 yd narrow gold rickrack or metallic trim
- Small amount potpourri
- Scissors and pencil

DIRECTIONS

PREPARE PIECES: For each ornament front, trace inner and outer lines of actual size pattern onto paper backing of fusible web. Following manufacturer's instructions, fuse web to wrong side of silk or lamé. Cut ornament front from fabric. Cut along inside line for window. Remove paper backing from web and fuse tulle to wrong side of ornament front. Trim tulle even with outer edges of ornament. Cut same shape piece of backing fabric for ornament back; do not cut along inside lines.

ORNAMENT FRONT: With metallic thread in needle and white thread in bobbin, work decorative machine stitches around window as desired. For ice cream cone ornament, stitch narrow rickrack around window.

ASSEMBLY: With wrong sides together, stitch front and back of ornament together along outside edge in small zigzag, leaving a small opening for filling with potpourri. With straight stitch, sew trim or rickrack over zigzag stitches, leaving a piece unstitched long enough to cover opening. Insert potpourri into opening. To make insertion easier, roll a sheet of paper into a cone. Slip narrow end into opening and pour potpourri into wider end. Zigzag opening closed. Stitch remaining trim in place over zigzag stitches. Cut a 7" length of trim or rickrack and fold in half. Tack to top of ornament for hanging loop.

THREAD: *Coats Dual Duty thread; Coats Gold Metallic thread*

- *Potpourri Star Pattern (actual size)*

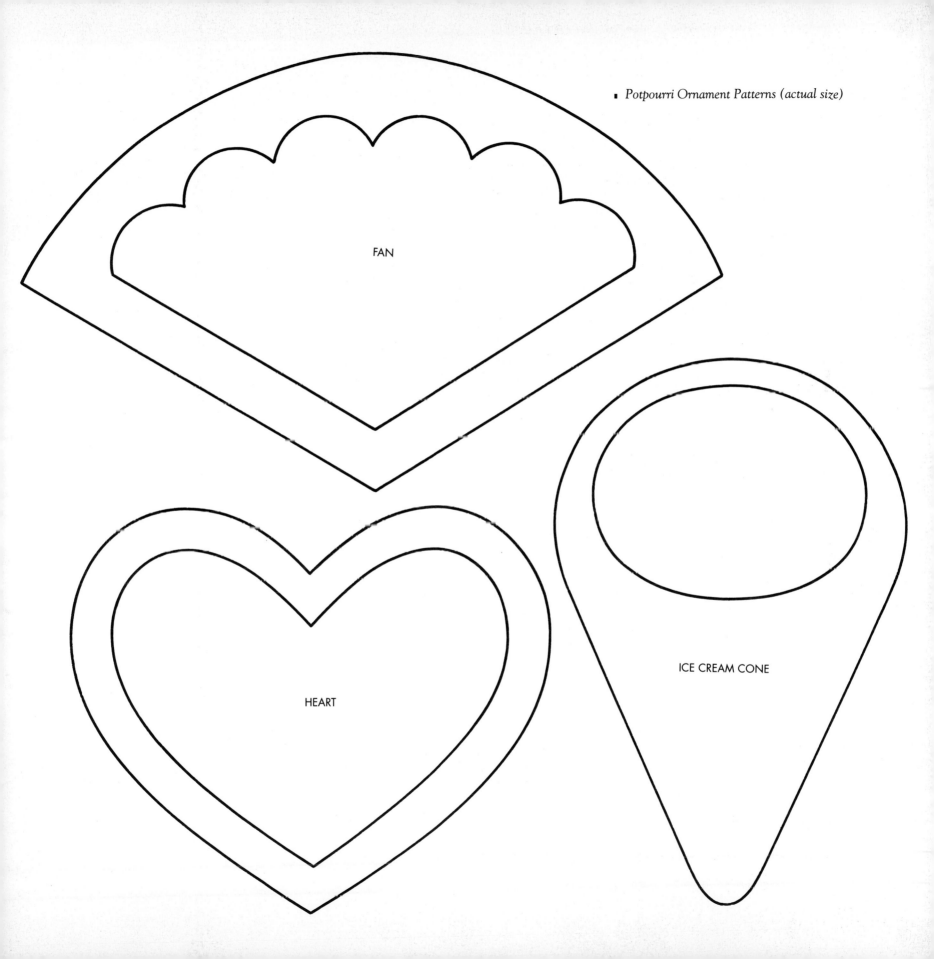

FAN

HEART

ICE CREAM CONE

■ *Potpourri Ornament Patterns (actual size)*

Stunning Stockings

Who wouldn't be excited to wake up on Christmas morning and discover a stocking full of goodies? Anyone would enjoy a favorite stocking that will forever evoke precious memories. Each stocking in this collection, hung by the chimney with care, is special enough to become such a cherished item. A Richly Ribboned Stocking, a patchwork Christmas Star Stocking, a brightly colored felt Folk Art Christmas Stocking, a cross-stitch Holly Heart Stocking, and a velvet and golden Celestial Boot—there is surely a future heirloom stocking here for someone dear to you.

RICHLY RIBBONED STOCKING

SIZE

- Stocking is 14½" high.

YOU WILL NEED

- ½ yd hunter green velvet
- ½ yd lining fabric
- 1 yd each five patterned ribbons, ½" to ¾" wide each
- 1¼ yd cording, for piping
- Matching thread
- Scissors, pencil, and paper

DIRECTIONS

PREPARE PIECES: Enlarge stocking pattern on page 45 (see page 21, "Enlarging Patterns"). Trace pattern onto paper, adding ½" seam allowance. Place pattern on velvet and cut out. Reverse pattern and cut

second stocking for back. Using pattern, cut two pieces from lining fabric, reversing one. From velvet, make a bias strip to cover piping, 1¼" wide and 1¼ yd long, piecing together as required. Cut a 4½" x 15" cuff from velvet and one the same size from lining fabric.

APPLIQUÉ RIBBONS: Using photo as a guide, pin one length of ribbon at an angle on center of stocking front. Machine stitch onto velvet. Continue to add ribbons to stocking front, parallel with first and ¼" apart until stocking front is covered. Trim ribbons along edge of stocking. Sew ribbons on velvet cuff piece, keeping ribbons parallel with long edge.

ASSEMBLY: With right sides together, place stocking front and stocking front lining together and sew across top. Repeat for backs. Turn right side out, folding along top seam so stocking pieces are even with stocking linings. Fold and stitch velvet bias strip over cording to make piping. Baste to stocking back, matching raw edges. With right sides together, sew stocking front to back, leaving top edge open. Trim curves and turn. Press lightly.

CUFF: With right sides together, sew cuff to cuff lining, keeping a short edge open for turning. Turn right side out.

FINISHING: Whipstitch cuff to upper edge of stocking, overlapping ends at center back. Sew overlapped ends. Cut a 5" length of ribbon. Fold in half and tack ends to top left hand corner of stocking back for hanging loop.

RIBBONS: *C.M. Offray and Son*

CHRISTMAS STAR STOCKING

SIZE

- Stocking is 15" high.

YOU WILL NEED

- Fabrics: ½ yd each ivory polished cotton, red solid cotton, green and white striped cotton; ¼ yd dark green pin dot cotton
- ½ yd low-loft quilt batting
- 1¼ yd cording, for piping
- Matching thread
- Scissors, straight edge, pencil, and cardboard
- Tracing paper for pattern

DIRECTIONS

PREPARE PIECES: Enlarge quilt pattern on page 40 (see page 21, "Enlarging Patterns"). Using tracing paper and pencil, trace star block patterns onto cardboard to use as templates, adding ¼" seam allowance throughout. Cut out. Following diagram and using templates, cut out pieces for two blocks. From ivory, cut out ten squares, each 4½". Cut two lining pieces and two batting pieces, each 12" x 16". From red fabric, cut one strip on straight grain, $1\frac{1}{2}$" x 8", for top border. Make a bias strip to cover piping, $1\frac{1}{4}$" wide and $1\frac{1}{4}$ yd long, piecing together as required. Cut one bias strip, 2" x 16", for top edge binding; one bias strip, 2" x 6", for loop; one bias strip, $2\frac{1}{2}$" x 4", for bow center; and two bias strips, $2\frac{1}{2}$" x 13", for bow. From green and white striped fabric, with stripes running vertically and perpendicular to long edges, cut one strip on grain, $2\frac{1}{2}$" x 8", for top border and one piece, 12" x 16", for stocking back. From dark green pin dot, cut one bias strip, $2\frac{1}{2}$" x 4", for bow center and two bias strips, $2\frac{1}{2}$" x 13", for bow.

PIECING: Following diagram on page 41, join star blocks together. Join a $4\frac{1}{2}$" square of ivory along side of star block, and another ivory square on opposite side of block. Repeat for second star block. Join these two strips together along long edge, staggering star block as shown on diagram. Join three ivory squares together in a strip and join to top of star blocks, following placement on diagram. Repeat along bottom edge.

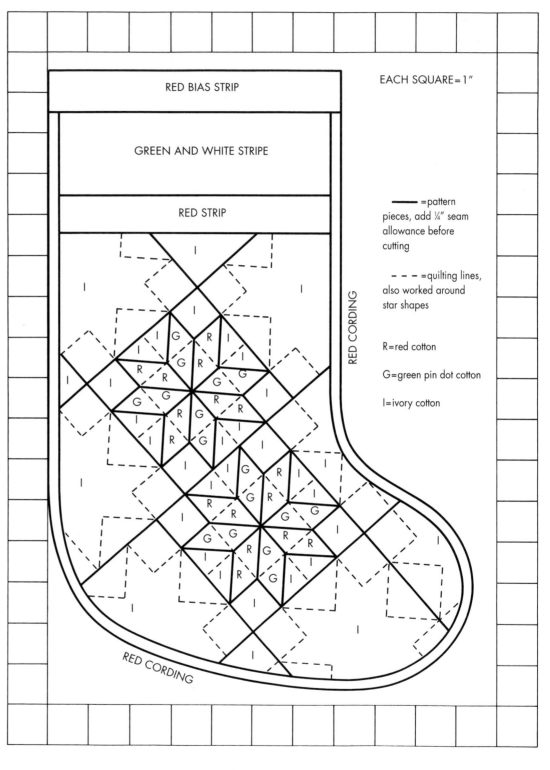

RED BIAS STRIP

GREEN AND WHITE STRIPE

RED STRIP

RED CORDING

RED CORDING

EACH SQUARE = 1"

——— = pattern pieces, add $\frac{1}{4}$" seam allowance before cutting

– – – = quilting lines, also worked around star shapes

R = red cotton

G = green pin dot cotton

I = ivory cotton

♦ ▪ *Christmas Star Stocking Quilt Pattern*

▪ *Christmas Star Stocking Piecing Diagram*

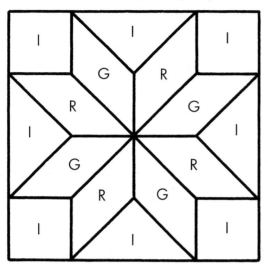

I=ivory, R=red, G=green

STOCKING FRONT: Using stocking pattern, cut out lower front. Join long edge of 1½" x 8" red strip to top of stocking front. Join long edge of 2½" x 8" green and white striped border to red strip.

QUILTING: Lay front lining on work surface. Center batting on lining, then place pieced front right side up on top. Beginning at center, baste layers together. Machine quilt around star of star block. Using star block pattern as a guide, mark and machine quilt same design on ivory blocks. Machine "stitch in the ditch" along top and lower seams of red strip. In same manner as front, layer green and white striped stocking back with quilt batting and ivory lining piece. Machine quilt vertical lines, 1" apart, across stocking back. Following pattern, cut out stocking front and back from quilted pieces, adding ½" seam allowance.

ASSEMBLY: Fold and stitch 1¼ yd red bias strip over cording to make piping. Baste to stocking back, matching raw edges. With right sides together, sew stocking front to

back, using basting as a guide. Trim curves and turn. Press lightly. Bind top edge with 2" x 16" red bias strip. For hanging loop, fold 2" x 6" red bias strip in half lengthwise and stitch. Turn right side out and zigzag ends together. Slipstitch to stocking back inside top left corner.

BOW: With right sides together, sew dark green pin dot bow bias strip to red bow bias strip, sewing one short end at 45-degree angle and leaving other end open. Trim seams and clip points; turn and press. In the same manner sew bow center together. Fold open ends of bow strips 3" in from end to form loops. Overlapping open ends of both strips, stitch across. Pinch small pleat in center and tack in place. Cover with bow center strip and slipstitch in place. Pin bow to front of stocking and slipstitch in place.

FOLK ART CHRISTMAS STOCKING

SIZE

▪ Stocking is 15" high.

YOU WILL NEED

- **Felt:** ⅓ yd each dark green and red; ¼ yd orange; 9" x 12" piece each bright green and magenta
- **Thread to match felt**
- **Wool tapestry yarn:** 2 skeins red; 1 skein magenta
- **Wooden beads with large hole for yarn:** 1 large orange; 2 medium orange; 3 medium red
- **1 yd paper-backed fusible transfer web**

- **Small sharp-pointed scissors**
- **Straight edge and pencil**
- **Tracing paper for pattern**
- **Large darning needle**

DIRECTIONS

PREPARE PATTERNS: Enlarge stocking and appliqué patterns on page 42 (see page 21, "Enlarging Patterns"). Using tracing paper and pencil, trace stocking pattern. Transfer appliqué shapes onto paper backing of fusible web, reversing tracing paper to mirror-image patterns. Extend cuff trellis appliqué pattern until 16" long. Transfer onto paper backing.

PREPARE PIECES: Following manufacturer's instructions and color key, fuse web to wrong side of felt. Cut out appliqués. From dark green felt, cut two stocking patterns and a 5" x 17" piece for cuff. From red, cut a stocking pattern, keeping top edge even and remaining sides ½" larger than dark green stocking. Cut a 6" x 17" piece for cuff.

APPLIQUÉ: Place dark green stocking front piece on ironing board and following pattern, lay design on stocking. Remove paper backings and iron appliqué shapes in place. Iron orange trellis appliqué on dark green cuff. Trim dark green even with orange trellis. Iron small hearts in place. Set sewing machine to small zigzag stitch and with matching threads, stitch around all shapes. With darning needle and magenta wool, work French knots (see page 31) on stocking front, following pattern.

ASSEMBLY: Pin wrong side of appliquéd stocking front to red felt stocking shape with top edges even and ½" of red felt extending along outside edges of stocking. Pin dark green stocking back to wrong side of red felt, keeping green front and back stocking edges even.

EACH SQUARE =1"

KEY

● =French knot

A=red

B=orange

C=bright green

D=magenta

E=dark green

With green thread in sewing machine, straight stitch around outside edges of stocking, leaving top edge open. Cut red felt into zigzag pattern. Pin wrong side of cuff appliqué to red felt, leaving ½" red felt extending along both long edges. With matching thread, zigzag stitch in place. Cut red felt in zigzag pattern. Cut a ¾" x 6" strip of red felt. Fold in half and tack to top of stocking for hanging loop. Lining up short edges at center of stocking back and cutting to fit, stitch cuff to top of stocking. Sew short edges together by hand.

TASSELS: Cut a 3" square of cardboard. Wrap red yarn around cardboard 50 times. With a 20" length of yarn folded in half, tie yarn together at one edge. Cut other edge. Wind second 20" length of yarn around tassel, 1" below top, and tie to secure. Make second tassel and tie closed. Thread yarn with beads, joining tassels together with large bead. Tack in place on front of stocking.

FUSIBLE WEB: *Pellon Wonder-Under Transfer Web*
TAPESTRY YARN: *DMC*

▪ *Folk Art Christmas Stocking Pattern*

HOLLY HEART STOCKING

SIZE

- Stocking is 14½" high.

YOU WILL NEED

- ½ yd Zweigart Valerie 20-count fabric, cream & metallic gold #118
- 1 skein each six-strand embroidery floss: dark red, medium red, light red, light green, medium green, dark green, darkest green, darkest red
- ½ yd cream satin fabric for lining
- ½ yd cream lace, 2" wide
- ¼ yd each ribbon, ⅛" wide, in red and cream
- ½ yd gold "Beads by the Yard"
- 4 gold 10mm jingle bells
- Embroidery hoop and needle
- Matching thread
- Scissors, pencil, and paper

COLOR KEY

ANCHOR		DMC	
45	◤	814	dark red
43	☒	815	medium red
979	—	312	light red
1042	•	504	light green
876	≡	503	medium green
877	■	502	dark green
683	—	500	darkest green (Outline for holly)
897	—	902	darkest red (Outline for berries and bow)

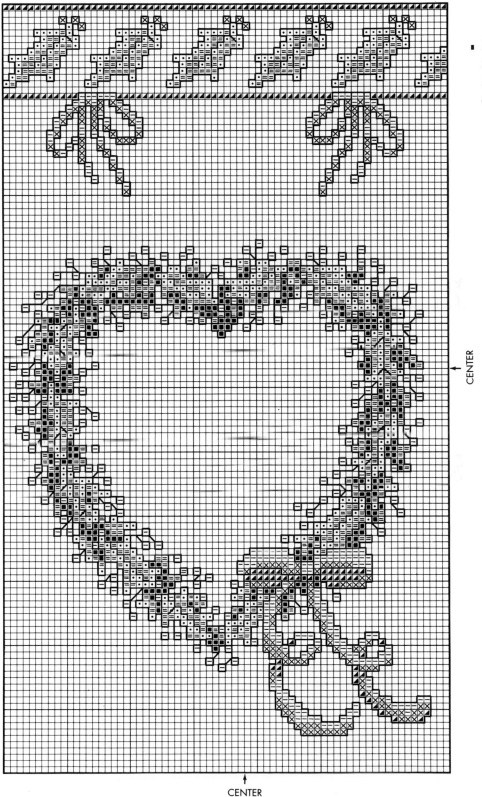

Holly Heart Stocking Chart

CENTER

CENTER

DIRECTIONS

CROSS-STITCHING: Cut 20-count fabric into 2 equal pieces large enough for stocking pattern. With contrasting thread, baste horizontal and vertical centers of fabric. Center design on fabric, matching fabric center with center of chart. Following chart and key, work cross-stitch with two strands of floss over two fabric threads (see page 17, "How to Cross-Stitch"). Work backstitch with one strand of floss, stitching around holly with darkest green and around berries and bow with darkest red. When embroidery is finished, hand wash fabric in cold water. Dry flat and press on a well-padded surface.

ASSEMBLY: Enlarge stocking pattern on page 45 (see page 21, "Enlarging Patterns"). Trace pattern for stocking onto paper, adding 1/2" seam allowance. Place pattern on embroidered fabric and cut out. Reverse pattern and cut second stocking for back. Using pattern, cut two pieces from lining fabric, reversing one. With right sides together, place front and front lining together and sew across top. Repeat for backs. Turn right side out, folding along top seam so stocking pieces are even with stocking linings. With right sides

together, sew stocking front to back, leaving top edge open. Trim curves and turn. Press lightly.

FINISHING: Whipstitch lace to upper edge of stocking, overlapping ends at center back. Whipstitch gold beads along lace edge. Cut two 5" lengths of each ribbon from red and cream. Holding one red and one cream piece together, fold in half and tack ends to top left corner of stocking back for hanging loop. Holding remaining two pieces together, tie a bow around hanging loop. Stitch bells on ribbon ends.

EMBROIDERY FLOSS: DMC

CELESTIAL BOOT

SIZE

- Stocking is 14 1/2" high.

YOU WILL NEED

- 1/2 yd blue velvet
- 1/2 yd blue cotton fabric for lining
- 1/4 yd gold quilted lamé for cuff and piping
- Star fruit or potato and star stencil
- Gold fabric paint
- 1" flat paint brush
- 1 1/4 yds white twisted cording, for piping
- 1 yd gold cording
- Matching thread
- 6" length gold-edged ribbon for hanging loop
- Scissors, pencil, paper, and paper towels

- *Star Stencil Pattern (actual size)*

DIRECTIONS

NOTE: If star fruit is not available when you plan to make this stocking, make a potato stamp with the star stencil pattern provided and use as star fruit is used.

STAR PRINTING: Cut star fruit in half. Place cut side down on paper towel to remove excess juice. Lay out velvet on flat surface. Brush star fruit with gold paint and place on velvet, pressing firmly, to print gold star. Repeat to make allover design. If necessary, use paint brush to touch up stars. Allow to dry thoroughly.

ASSEMBLY: Enlarge pattern on page 45 (see page 21). Trace pattern onto paper, adding 1/2" seam allowance. Place pattern on painted fabric and cut out. Reverse pattern and cut second stocking for back. Using pattern, cut two pieces from lining fabric, reversing one. From lamé, make a bias strip to cover piping, 1 1/4" wide and 1 1/4 yd long, piecing together as required. With right sides together, place painted front piece and front lining together and sew across top. Repeat for backs. Turn right side out, folding along top seam so stocking pieces are even with stocking linings. Fold and stitch lamé bias strip over cording to make

EACH SQUARE = 1"

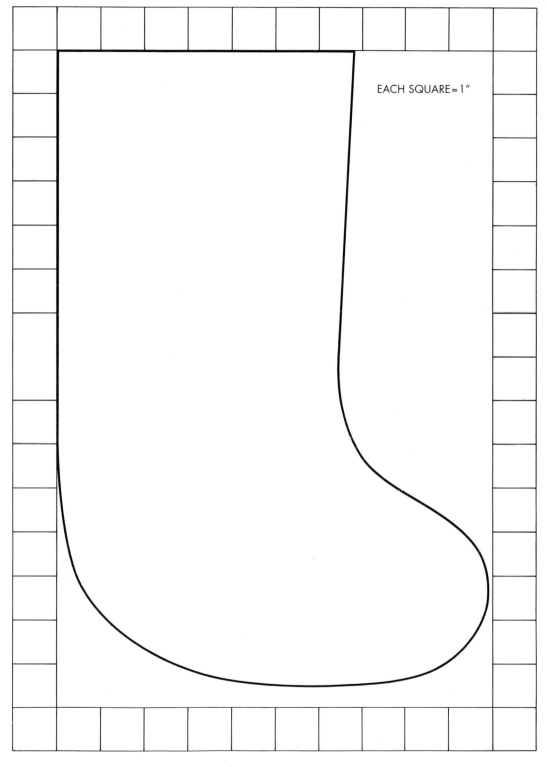

piping. Baste to stocking back, matching raw edges. With right sides together, sew stocking front to back, leaving top edge open. Trim curves and turn. Press lightly, using a pressing cloth.

CUFF: From lamé, cut two pieces, each 4½" x 15". With right sides together, sew around cuff, leaving one short edge open for turning. Turn right side out.

FINISHING: Whipstitch cuff to upper edge of stocking, overlapping ends at center back. Sew overlapped ends. Whipstitch gold cording along both long edges. Fold ribbon in half and tack ends to top left hand corner of stocking back for hanging loop.

▪ *Stocking Pattern for Richly Ribboned Stocking, Holly Heart Stocking, and Celestial Boot*

REINDEER TREE SKIRT

This tree skirt may look complicated but is deceptively easy to create. The appliqués are ironed on, and the "stitching" is actually paint. Bordered in a checkered pattern and trimmed with giant rickrack, this festive tree skirt will dress the tree beautifully.

SIZE

- Tree skirt is approximately 52" in diameter.

YOU WILL NEED

- 1½ yds 60" wide red wool fabric
- ¾ yd 60" wide off-white wool fabric
- ½ yd 60" wide green wool fabric
- 2 yds paper-backed fusible web
- 5 yds red jumbo rickrack
- Fabric glue
- 3 bottles each 1oz fabric writers in red and green
- Small sharp-pointed scissors
- Straight edge, pencil, or vanishing marker

DIRECTIONS

PREPARE PIECES: Enlarge patterns (see page 21). Trace four reindeer facing left and four reindeer facing right onto paper backing of fusible web. Trace four trees. On a 6" x 43" strip of fusible web, draw 116 squares, each 1½". On 10½" x 24" strip of fusible web, draw 112 squares, each 1½". Cut out. Following manufacturer's instructions, fuse eight reindeer and 116 squares to white fabric. Fuse four trees and 112 squares to green fabric. Cut out appliqués. On wrong side of red fabric, draw an octagon with each side measuring 20" and with a 52" diameter. Cut out octagon.

APPLIQUÉ: Referring to photograph, peel off paper backing and fuse 104 squares each of green and white around outside edges of red fabric in checkerboard pattern, trimming squares to miter at corners and working along one edge at a time. Alternating three white squares with two green squares, fuse squares to make a diamond pattern, positioning five along every other side of octagon, 2" in from checkerboard pattern. Fuse tree, 2" in from each center white diamond. Fuse two reindeer facing each other on either side of each tree. Draw a 7" diameter circle in center of red fabric for hole for tree trunk. Draw a line from center of circle, straight through center of tree motif, center of white diamond, and checkerboard patterns on one side for back opening. Cut along line and cut out center circle.

FINISHING: Outline reindeer and white diamonds with red fabric writer. Outline trees and green diamonds with green fabric writer. Outline checkerboard with green fabric writer. Glue rickrack in place around outside edges of octagon, easing around corners and beginning and ending along back opening. Using red fabric writer, paint along edges of back opening and around center circle.

FUSIBLE WEB: *Pellon Wonder-Under Transfer Web*

EACH SQUARE = 1"

- *Reindeer Tree Skirt Patterns*

FATHER CHRISTMAS SHADOW BOX

A shadow box filled with special Christmas treasures captures the excitement and fascination of the holiday in small, endearing scenes. Dried flowers gathered during the summer (or available at floral and crafts shops) provide a rainbow of color. Add special handcrafted objects and collectibles to create a one-of-a-kind holiday display.

SIZE

- Shadow box is 12" x 18" x 2".

YOU WILL NEED

FOR SHADOW BOX:

- Shadow box #105-V from Mueller-Wood Kraft, Inc. (see Sources)
- 2 yds 1" wide red grosgrain ribbon for outer edges
- 2 yds twisted red and gold cording for front

FOR GIFT BOXES:

- 2 small dollhouse wrapped packages to fit desired section

FOR ROCKING HORSE:

- Unpainted dollhouse rocking horse
- 1 small Christmas bear

FOR BASKET:

- Small basket
- Boxwood greens, red berries, and white stattice

FOR BIRDHOUSE:

- Unpainted dollhouse birdhouse
- 3 small red birds
- Sponge

FOR DRIED FLOWER SECTIONS:

- 1 block floral foam
- Assorted dried flowers such as chrysanthe-

mums, hill flowers, roses, and stattice to fill boxes
- Small pine cones
- Kitchen knife

FOR SANTA:
- 2 pieces white velvet, each 4" x 7"
- Small amount of polyester stuffing
- Black permanent marker
- Dressmaker's carbon paper

FOR CHRISTMAS TREE:
- Purchased wire-tipped greens
- 1 floral stick, 4" long
- Red and gold flower-shaped sequins
- Small basket

FOR HEARTS:
- 3 small wooden hearts, each 1¼"
- Small piece of cardboard

FOR TEDDY BEARS:
- 3 small Christmas bears
- Dollhouse Christmas stockings
- Dollhouse red ladder
- Assorted small dollhouse wrapped packages

MISCELLANEOUS:
- 2oz bottle each red, white, gold, and green paint writers
- Scissor, straight edge, and pencil
- Hot glue gun and glue sticks
- ½" flat bristle paintbrush and small pointed paintbrush for details

DIRECTIONS

SHADOW BOX: Glue red ribbon around outside edge of box. Glue twisted cording around front of box. Paint front edges of section partitions with two coats of red.

GIFT BOXES: Fit gift boxes into section and glue in place.

ROCKING HORSE: Paint rocking horse red. Let dry. Paint flowers and designs as desired. Glue bear to rocking horse. Glue rocking horse in place.

BASKET: Paint basket with two coats of red. Paint basket rim with two coats of gold. Glue boxwood greens, berries, and stattice in basket. Glue basket in place.

BIRDHOUSE: Paint birdhouse with two coats of white. Using sponge, dab green paint on sides of birdhouse for a mottled effect. Paint roof edges green. Using sponge, thinly spread green paint across roof for a streaky effect. Glue birds to birdhouse. Glue birdhouse in place.

DRIED FLOWER SECTIONS: Cut floral foam 1" deep and the size to fit sections that will be filled with flowers and pinecones. Break flower stems so flower is just below surface of box when pushed into foam to secure. Tightly fill sections with flowers or pine cones as desired.

SANTA: Transfer Santa pattern to back of one piece of white velvet for Santa front. Reverse pattern and transfer Santa pattern, adding ¼" seam allowance to back of second piece of velvet for Santa back. Cut out. With right sides together and using ¼" seam allowance, sew around outside edge of Santa, leaving lower edge open for stuffing. Trim curves and turn. Stuff. Sew opening closed. Paint details of Santa as shown on pattern. Mix small amount of white and red paint for Santa's face. Use black permanent marker for small details in fur, face, and hair. Glue Santa in place.

CHRISTMAS TREE: Wrap wired greens around floral stick to make Christmas tree. Glue sequins to greens; glue tree into basket. Glue basket in place in same section as Santa.

HEARTS: Paint one heart each in green, white, and red. Using gold paint writer, add detail patterns as desired. Cut three strips of cardboard ½" wide and 2" long. Bend each end of cardboard back ½". Glue one end to the back of each heart. Glue other end of cardboard in place on back of section.

TEDDY BEARS: Glue one bear in place on ladder. Glue ladder in place. Glue stockings on walls of section. Arrange packages and remaining two bears in box and glue in place.

- *Santa Pattern (actual size)*

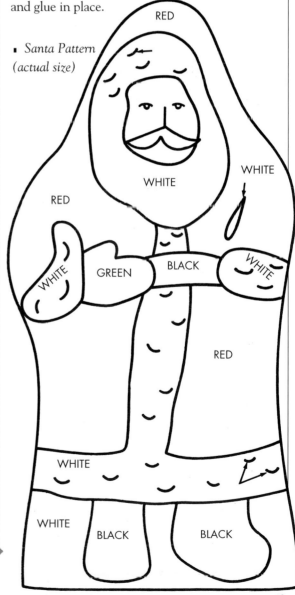

Gifts from the Heart

HAVE YOU EVER WISHED THAT YOU COULD MAKE ALL THE CHRISTMAS GIFTS YOU GIVE? HANDMADE GIFTS ARE SO SPECIAL AND APPRECIATED. IT IS POSSIBLE TO MAKE QUITE A FEW GIFTS BY SETTING TIME ASIDE DURING THE MONTHS BEFORE CHRISTMAS. HERE ARE NUMEROUS WONDERFUL, FUN-TO-MAKE, FUN-TO-GIVE GIFT IDEAS.

FRUITFUL SLEIGH

This charming painted sleigh reflects all the bounty of Nature. Filled with tiny wrapped gifts, artificial fruit, or dried flowers, it is a festive centerpiece for a holiday celebration. But its beauty extends year-round, making it a lovely gift for someone special. The sleigh, available by mail order, is ready-to-paint. The runners are attached later.

SIZE

- Sleigh is 9" x 16".

YOU WILL NEED

- 9" x 16" unfinished sleigh available from Wooden Hen Manufacturing (see Sources), with choice of wooden or metal runners
- Artist brushes: #10 or #12 flat for large fruit, #2 or #4 for dry brushing, #5 round for grapes, and #3 round for lines and veins
- Acrylic paints: 2oz bottles, 1 each of burgundy, pueblo red, light green, muted purple, colonial green, soft black, yellow, and country red
- Black rustproof paint for metal runners
- 1 bottle of pickling stain, rose
- 1 bottle of antiquing solution
- Fine sandpaper and tack cloth
- Tracing paper and transfer paper
- Double-edged stylus, pencil, and tape
- Screwdriver
- 1" foam paintbrush
- Paper towels and brown paper bags
- Acrylic satin finish spray sealer and varnish

DIRECTIONS

NOTE: One "part" is a dollop the size of an M&M candy. Allow all paints and sealers to dry thoroughly between coats.

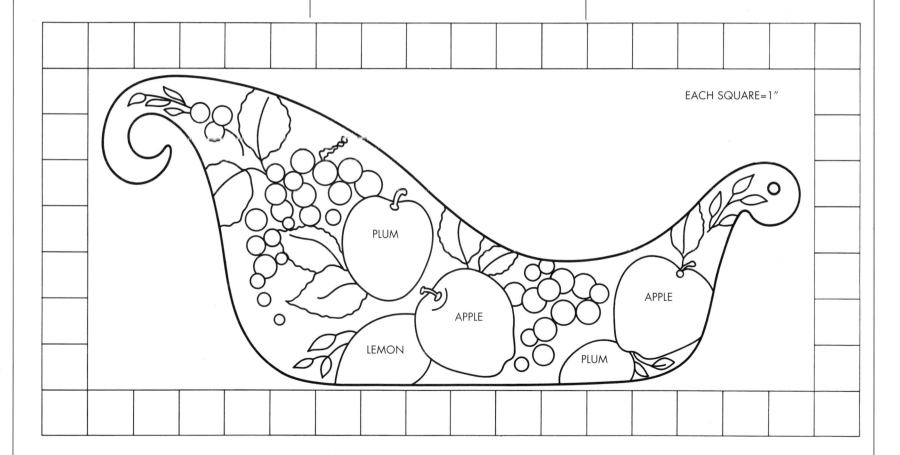

EACH SQUARE=1"

PLUM

APPLE

LEMON

APPLE

PLUM

- *Fruitful Sleigh Pattern*

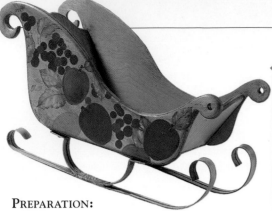

PREPARATION:
Lightly sand wood and clean with tack cloth. Spray with two coats of sealer. Lightly sand runners. Paint with two coats of black. With foam brush, paint sleigh with two coats of pickling stain, sanding with brown paper bag between coats. Let piece cure for 48 hours.

PAINT FRUIT DESIGN: Enlarge pattern (see page 21, "Enlarging Patterns"). Using tracing paper, transfer paper, and stylus, transfer design onto sides of sleigh. Paint grapes with two coats of burgundy. Repaint seven to nine grapes with pueblo red. Mix five parts light green with one-half part purple and paint large veined leaves with two coats. While second coat is still damp, outline leaves with purple. When leaves are dry, paint veins with purple. Highlight leaves with colonial green or light green, as desired, using #2 or #4 flat brush and dry brushing with a small amount of paint. Paint small unveined leaves with two coats of colonial green. Paint plums with two coats of purple. Shade plums with a mixture of one part soft black and one part purple. Use same mixture to paint stems. Paint lemon with two coats of a mixture of five parts yellow and one-quarter part purple. Add one part purple to yellow mixture to shade lemon. Paint apples with two coats of country red. Mix one-half part country red with one part burgundy and one-eighth part soft black to shade apples. Paint edge of sleigh with one coat of light green. Paint runners with one coat of light green. When dry, use worn sandpaper to lightly sand runners, allowing small amount of black to show through. Paint and sand runners with second coat of light green in same manner as before.

FINISHING: Attach runners to sleigh. Spray paint sleigh and runners with sealer. Following manufacturer's instructions, apply antiquing solution. Remove with clean paper towels to keep from redepositing solution. When dry, apply two or three coats of varnish.

GARDEN DREAMS LAP DESK

Summer gardens will bloom all year long wherever this magnificent decoupage lap desk is planted! An unpainted pine lap desk is the background for favorite floral and strawberry wrapping paper that has been carefully cut out and glued. The inside is lined with a coordinating marbleized paper and makes a perfect spot for storing special stationery, diaries, and writing tools.

This decoupage technique works well on any unfinished wood box and the wide assortment of wrapping papers available offers limitless possibilities for variations on this theme. Lap desks and boxes can be purchased at any crafts store or an unfinished furniture resource.

SIZE
- Unfinished pine lap desk is 15" wide, 11" deep, 3" in front, and 4½" in back.

YOU WILL NEED
- Unfinished pine lap desk or box
- Black acrylic paint
- Acrylic gel medium
- 1 sheet of desired patterned gift wrap or other paper images
- 1 sheet of marbleized paper for lining
- Glue stick and craft glue
- Cuticle or embroidery scissors and pencil
- 1" foam brush and ½" flat bristle brush
- Fine sandpaper and tack cloth
- Acrylic satin finish spray sealer

DIRECTIONS
DECOUPAGE: Lightly sand lap desk and clean with tack cloth. Paint with two coats of black paint, allowing to dry between coats. Using small, sharp scissors, cut out images from gift wrap or other source, carefully removing background color. Apply a dab of glue stick to the back of each image and, referring to photo, position design on desk. Position largest or most important images first. When design is arranged on all sides, and working with one image at a time, brush gel medium onto back of image and position on desk. Rub image with finger to remove any air bubbles. Attach all remaining images. Let dry thoroughly. Spray with two coats of sealer.

DESK LINING: Cut sheets of marbleized paper to fit all inside surfaces of desk. Glue in place.

CENTER

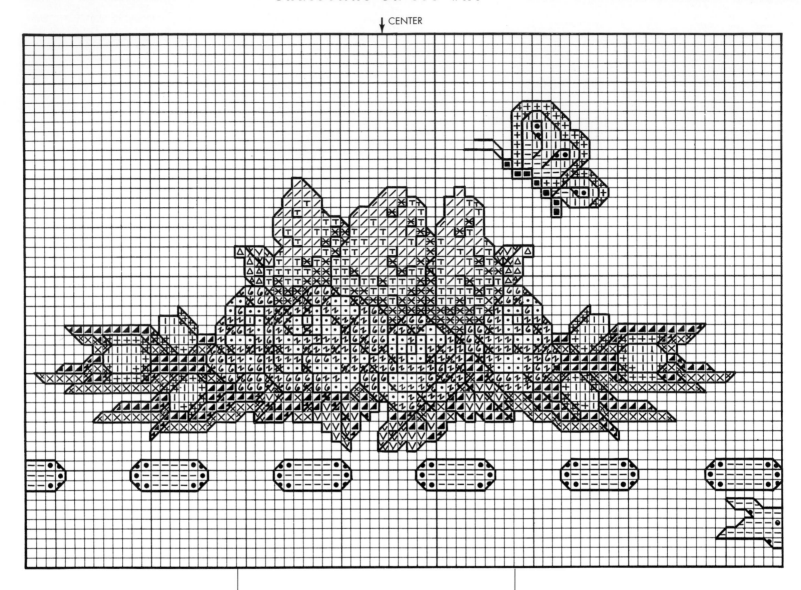

FLOWERS, BOWS, AND BUTTERFLIES DRESSER TRAY

Inspired by summer flowers, this feminine dresser tray would make an ideal present for a sister, mother, daughter, or dear friend. Pretty floral and ribbon motifs are cross-stitched on crisp white linen, set off by an oval mat and protected by glass. The unfinished tray is available by mail and can be painted white or a shade that suits the room of the lucky recipient of this thoughtful gift.

SIZE

- Tray is 12" x 19".

YOU WILL NEED

- Six-strand embroidery floss: 2 skeins antique blue light; 1 skein each salmon very light, salmon, thistle light, thistle medium, thistle dark, antique blue medium, antique blue dark, parrot green light, parrot green medium, parrot green, grass green dark, topaz light, topaz medium light, and tawny very dark
- 12"x19" piece 28-count white linen fabric
- Embroidery hoop and needle
- Masking tape
- 12"x19" tray: Classic Tray #60106 from Sudberry House (see Sources)
- 12"x19" blue mat board, with 9"x15" oval window cut in center
- Paintbrush and white paint
- Spray-on varnish

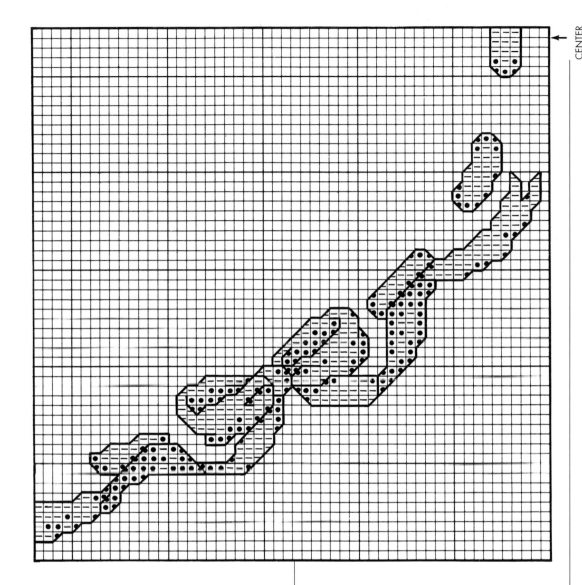

← CENTER

COLOR KEY

DMC		ANCHOR	
3712	•	1020	salmon very light
760	↙	1022	salmon
3328	6	1024	thistle light
341	∕	117	thistle medium
340	T	118	thistle dark
333	✕	119	antique blue light
932	—	1033	antique blue medium
931	●	1034	antique blue dark
3348	V	254	parrot green light
907	∧	255	parrot green medium
905	◢	257	parrot green
986	✕	245	grass green dark
725			305	topaz light
783	+	306	topaz medium light
3021	■	905	tawny very dark
	—		Outline stitch in tawny very dark

DIRECTIONS

CROSS-STITCHING: Tape edges of linen with masking tape to prevent raveling. With contrasting thread, baste horizontal and vertical centers of fabric. Center design on fabric, matching fabric center with center of chart. Continue border motif around all outside edges and work bow motif in each corner, reversing chart for mirror image. Following chart and key, work cross-stitch with two strands of floss over two threads (see page 17). Use one strand of floss for back stitch. When

embroidery is finished, hand wash fabric in cold water. Dry flat and press on a well-padded surface.

FINISHING: Following manufacturer's instruction, assemble tray. Paint with several coats of white paint, allowing to dry throughly between coats. Spray with two coats of varnish. Following manufacturer's instructions, mount linen in tray, centering design. Cover with mat board and glass.

◆ **EMBROIDERY FLOSS:** *Anchor*

▪ *Flowers, Bows, and Butterflies Dresser Tray Chart*

TARTAN DESK SET

It's not always easy to come up with original gift ideas for the men in your life. This masculine fabric-covered desk set would make a handsome addition to any gentleman's study or home office. While the tartan fabric gives a crisp look and is easy to work with, a foulard pattern or paisley would also be appropriate. Easy-to-follow instructions can be adapted to other items such as photo albums, date books, or file folders.

SIZES

- Blotter is 16¼" x 21½". Accordian file is 10" x 12". Three-ring binder is 11½" high. Large book is 7½" x 9½". Small book is 4½" x 7". Large frame is 10" x 12". Small frame is 7" x 9". File box is 4" deep x 4¾" high x 6½" wide. Pencil jar is 4½" high. Clipboard is 9" x 12½".

YOU WILL NEED

FOR ALL PROJECTS:
- 3 yds paper-backed fusible web
- Scissor, straight edge, and pencil
- Spray glue or white craft glue
- 3 yds each of two contrasting plaid fabrics

FOR BLOTTER:
- 16¼" x 21½" blotter
- 2 matching pieces 5½" x 20¼" fabric cut from same plaid
- Black construction paper: 1 piece 16¼" x 16½" for top; 1 piece 16¼" x 21½" for back

FOR ACCORDIAN FILE:
- 10" x 12" accordian file
- 2 matching pieces 12" x 14" fabric cut from same plaid
- 1 yd ⅜" wide black grosgrain ribbon

FOR 3-RING BINDER:
- 3-ring binder 11½" high with 1½" spine
- 1 piece 13½" x 25" plaid fabric
- 2 pieces 10" x 11" red construction paper

FOR LARGE BOOK:
- 7½" x 9½" notebook
- 1 piece 11½" x 17½" plaid fabric
- 2 pieces 6½" x 9" blue construction paper

FOR SMALL BOOK:
- 5" x 8" notebook
- 1 piece 10" x 13" plaid fabric
- 2 pieces 4½" x 7" blue construction paper

FOR LARGE FRAME:
- 8" x 10" frame with cardboard mat
- 1 piece 10" x 12" plaid fabric
- Blue paint and paintbrush

FOR SMALL FRAME:
- 5" x 7" frame with cardboard mat
- 1 piece 7" x 9" plaid fabric
- Green paint and paintbrush

FOR FILE BOX:
- 4" deep x 4¾" high x 6½" wide file box
- Fabric cut from same plaid: 1 piece 8½" x 9" for top; 2 matching pieces 2½" x 4" for top sides; 1 piece 5" x 8½" for bottom; 1 piece 4" x 4" for bottom sides
- 1 piece 4" x 6½" black construction paper
- 1 piece 22" blue braid trim

FOR PENCIL JAR:

- Empty, clean 4$1/2$" high can
- 1 piece 5$1/2$" x 11$1/2$" plaid fabric
- 1 piece 4$1/2$" x 11" black construction paper
- 1 piece 11" red woven trim

FOR CLIPBOARD:

- 9" x 12$1/2$" clipboard
- 1 piece 11" x 14$1/2$" plaid fabric
- 1 piece 9" x 12$1/2$" green construction paper

DIRECTIONS

BLOTTER: Measure and draw each side portion of blotter onto paper backing of fusible web. Add 1" to one long edge for inner edge margin of side panel, 2" to opposite long edge for outer edge margin, and 2" to each short edge for top and bottom edge margins. Cut out and center on wrong side of plaid fabrics, referring to photo and matching plaids. Following manufacturer's instructions, fuse onto fabric. Remove paper backing and place fabric on side portions of blotter, keeping margins. Clip fabric and turn top, bottom, and outside edge margins to wrong side of blotter, folding corners neatly. Lightly press to fuse in place. Fold inside edge margin and tuck under side panel and fuse in place. Glue 16$1/4$" x 16$1/2$" black construction paper in place on center of blotter, tucking under side panel. Glue 16$1/4$" x 21$1/2$" black construction paper in place on back.

ACCORDIAN FILE: Draw two rectangles, 10" x 12" each, on paper backing of fusible web. Fold 1" in on all edges of plaid fabric to wrong side and press. Following manufacturer's instructions, fuse web onto wrong side of fabric. Cut ribbon in half. Glue one end of one half to top of front and one end of other half to top of back for ties. Cut ends at an angle. Remove paper backing and fuse plaid pieces to front and back of accordian file, covering ends of ribbon.

3-RING BINDER: Open binder flat and trace around it on paper backing of fusible web, adding 1" on all sides. Cut out. Following manufacturer's instructions, fuse. Remove paper backing and center on binder. Clip corners and fold 1" to inside of binder. Lightly press to fuse in place, folding corners neatly. Glue construction paper on inside of binder to cover raw edges.

LARGE BOOK: Open notebook flat and trace around it onto paper backing of fusible web, adding 1" on all sides. Cut out. Following manufacturer's instructions, fuse onto wrong side of fabric. Remove paper backing and center on notebook. Clip corners and fold 1" to inside of book. Lightly press to fuse in place, folding corners neatly. Glue blue construction paper on inside of notebook to cover raw edges.

SMALL BOOK: Work same as for large book.

LARGE FRAME: Remove cardboard mat from frame. Using cardboard as a template, trace around both inside and outside edges onto paper backing of fusible web, adding 1" on all edges. Cut out. Following manufacturer's instructions, fuse onto wrong side of fabric. Cut out center and clip into corners. Remove paper backing and fuse fabric onto cardboard mat, folding margins to wrong side. Paint frame blue and let dry. Reassemble frame.

SMALL FRAME: Work same as for large frame, painting frame green.

FILE BOX: Cut fusible web, one piece, 8$1/2$"x 9" for top; one piece, 5"x 8$1/2$" for bottom back; one piece 4$1/2$"x 8$1/2$" for bottom front; two pieces, 2$1/2$"x 4" for top sides; two pieces, 4"x 4" for bottom sides. Center fusible web on wrong side of plaids, referring to photo and matching patterns. Following manufacturer's instructions, fuse in place. Remove paper backing and clip into corners. Fuse top front, top, and top back in place, folding margins over to sides. Fuse top sides in place, turning margin into box inside. Fuse box bottom, front, back, and sides in place, folding margins into box insides on front. Use glue to secure fabric in areas that iron cannot reach. Glue blue braid in place around edge of box top. Glue black construction paper to box bottom to cover raw edges.

PENCIL JAR: Measure height and circumference of empty can. Add 1" to each measurement and draw onto paper backing of fusible web. Following manufacturer's instructions, fuse onto wrong side of plaid fabric. Remove paper backing and fuse to can, overlapping short edges 1" and folding long edge margins to inside of can. Glue black construction paper to inside of can, covering raw edges. Glue red trim around top and bottom edges of can.

CLIPBOARD: Trace around clipboard onto paper backing of fusible web, adding 1" on all sides. Cut out. Following manufacturer's instructions, fuse web onto wrong side of plaid. Remove paper backing and, clipping into corners and fabric to fit around metal clip, fuse in place. Fold margin to wrong sides and, mitering corners, fuse in place. Cut green construction paper to fit back and glue in place to cover raw edges.

FUSIBLE WEB: Pellon Wonder-Under Transfer Web

FAMILY PHOTO FRAMES

As we add to our collections of family photos, the need for frames to display them grows with the generations. Framed photos or artwork make great personalized gifts—especially when the frame is handmade by the giver! This collection includes several looks and techniques that can get the whole family involved. Wood-burning is safe and simple to do, a project that could involve Dad and the older kids. Paint combing is fun and uses a simple homemade cardboard comb. We've chosen gold buttons for our Button Frame, but you could also use beads, colored stones, or fake jewels for an equally fabulous effect. Similarly, with the Gold Collage Frame, use favorite found or collected objects to personalize the frame. And, for the Sea Collage Frame, have the young ones begin gathering shells this summer and make frames to give to their grandparents at Christmas.

SIZES

- Assorted picture frames.

YOU WILL NEED

FOR ALL PROJECTS:
- 2" wide flat wooden picture frame
- Metal ruler and pencil
- Acrylic satin finish spray sealer

FOR WOOD-BURNED CHECKERBOARD FRAME:
- Wood-burning tool
- Red acrylic paint
- $1/2$" flat bristle paintbrush

FOR WOOD-BURNED AFRICAN-INSPIRED FRAME:
- Wood-burning tool

FOR COMBED FRAME:
- Gold acrylic paint
- Red acrylic paint
- 1" foam paintbrush
- Poster board
- Craft knife

FOR BUTTON FRAME:
- Gold acrylic paint
- Approximately 100 assorted metal buttons
- Hot glue gun and glue sticks

FOR GOLD COLLAGE FRAME:
- Gold acrylic paint or 2 to 3 squares of gold leaf (available from art supply stores)
- Assorted pressed metal decorations (available from crafts shops): 10 faux gold coins; 2 grape clusters; 2 gold crowns; 1 heraldic emblem; 2 pressed gold leaves; a 2" gold filigree square
- Hot glue gun and glue sticks

FOR SEA COLLAGE FRAME:
- Assorted sea-inspired motif decorations (available from crafts shops): 2 starfish in yellow and green; 1 turquoise star; 3 fish shapes, 2 seaweed shapes, 1 orange shell shape; $81/2$" round gold studs
- Hot glue gun and glue sticks
- Blue acrylic paint and sponge

DIRECTIONS

WOOD-BURNED CHECKERBOARD FRAME: With ruler and pencil, mark frame into $1/2$" squares. Using wood-burning tool and following manufacturer's instructions, burn pencil lines onto frame. To keep lines straight, run wood-burning tool along metal ruler. Mix small amount of red paint with water to make a wash stain. With paintbrush, paint every alternate square with red mixture. Paint sides with red mixture. Let dry. Spray with two coats of sealer.

WOOD-BURNED AFRICAN-INSPIRED FRAME: With ruler and pencil, mark 2" square in each corner. Draw smaller square $1/2$" inside of first square. Following photograph, draw lines connecting these two squares. Draw $3/4$" square in center and a small "x" in center of square. Divide sides into evenly spaced zigzag lines. Draw small triangle in each zigzag. Using wood-burning tool and following manufacturer's instructions, burn design in frame. To keep lines straight, run wood-burning tool along metal ruler. Burn lines on sides of frame. Spray with two coats of sealer.

COMBED FRAME: Cut a 4" x $13/4$" wide piece of poster board for comb. Mark short side into $1/4$" square sections. Cut out alternate sections to make comb. Paint frame with two coats of gold paint, allowing to dry between coats. Paint frame with one coat of red. While red paint is still wet, run comb across all four sides, overlapping comb marks in corners. Run comb across with sure straight strokes. Let dry. Spray with two coats of sealer.

BUTTON FRAME: Paint frame with two coats of gold paint, allowing to dry between coats. Arrange buttons around frame, covering surface. Glue buttons in place, pressing firmly to secure. Spray with two coats of sealer.

GOLD COLLAGE FRAME: Paint frame with two coats of gold paint, allowing to dry between coats. If using gold leaf, follow manufacturer's instructions to apply. Arrange decorations on gold frame. Glue decorations in place, pressing firmly to secure. Spray with two coats of sealer.

SEA COLLAGE FRAME: Sponge paint frame with blue. Let dry. Arrange sea motifs and gold studs on frame. Glue decorations in place, pressing firmly to secure. Spray with two coats of sealer.

CHRISTMAS COOKING

PART

2

The
holiday
season is the
time for warm reunions
with family, for writing chatty
cards to long-distance friends, for
tree-trimming, and for giving gifts from
your kitchen and from your heart. Get an
early start this year and, while big ripe strawberries,
tomatoes, peaches, and plums are in the market or in
your garden, stock your pantry and freezer with a variety of
homemade treats—from colorful preserved fruits to spicy chutneys and
nose-tingling pestos. Prepare handy mixes to whip together delicious waffles,
cornbread or warm, chewy oatmeal cookies on cold winter days. With confidence
and poise, you'll be pre-
pared to whip together
family meals, entertain
guests, and gather
homemade items to fill
gourmet gift baskets.

CHAPTER 1

Jams, Marmalades, and Preserved Fruits

PANCAKES SMOTHERED IN TART RED PLUM JAM. GINGERBREAD MEN GLAZED WITH GINGER-LEMON JELLY. SCONES SPREAD WITH ENGLISH LEMON CURD. SUNSHINE ORANGE SLICES AS AN ACCOMPANIMENT TO A HOLIDAY HAM. THESE ARE BUT A FEW OF THE DELICIOUS

OPTIONS AVAILABLE DURING THE CHRISTMAS SEASON, ESPE-CIALY IF YOU PLAN AHEAD AND MAKE THE JAMS, JELLIES, AND PRESERVES NOW WHILE THE FRUITS ARE AT THEIR RIPEST. BRING A TOUCH OF SUMMER TO YOUR WINTER TABLE WITH THESE MOUTHWATERING RECIPES.

CANNING JAMS, JELLIES, PRESERVES, PICKLES, AND SAUCES

EQUIPMENT LIST

- **6- to 8-quart kettle**—Made of heavy stainless steel or heavy enameled iron (aluminum and copper are not recommended because they react with acids in foods). Use for sterilizing jars and cooking foods.
- **Water bath canner**—A kettle with a rack for holding canning jars that is large enough to accommodate jars without them touching each other or the sides of the kettle and deep enough that jars can be covered by at least 1 inch of boiling water. Use for processing filled jars to sterilize and preserve contents.

    If you don't have a hot-water bath canner, you can use a very large stockpot, observing these precautions: The jars must not touch the bottom or sides of the pot—use a flat steamer rack on the bottom of the pot; the jars must not touch each other; and there must be enough space for the jars to be covered by 1 inch of water during the boiling process.
- **Preserving jars, lids, and rings**—For maximum safety, use only regular and wide-mouth jars with screw bands (or rings) and dome lids when preserving foods. The most useful sizes are half-pint, pint, and quart. Check jars carefully for cracks and chips—even a deep scratch

can cause the jar to break when it's filled. Use only new dome lids from the current year; they cannot be re-used. Rings can be re-used, however, if they are not scratched, bent, or rusted.

- **Wide-mouth funnel**—Useful for filling jars without dripping onto jar lip.
- **Tongs or jar lifter**—Needed for lifting hot jars.
- **Long-handled ladle and wooden spoons**—Handy for stirring and dipping hot preserves and jams.
- **Large and small knives and cutting board**—For preparing fruits and vegetables. Some recipes recommend a food processor or blender to make preparation quicker.

DIRECTIONS

To get started, first assemble all the equipment and ingredients you will need.

If you're making jams, preserves, pickles, sauces, or chutneys, thoroughly wash and rinse the jars and rings; turn the jars upside down to drain until you need them. Prepare lids following the manufacturer's directions.

If you're making any jelly or other foods to be water-bath processed for less than 10 minutes, you must sterilize the jelly jars and lids: Put the jars in a large pan or kettle and cover with water. Cover the pan and boil over low to medium heat for 10 minutes. Remove pan from heat and leave the jars in hot water until ready to use. Follow manufacturer's directions for lids.

Never shortcut processing or cooking times, and follow instructions carefully. Beware, too, of old tales, such as adding aspirin to preserve foods. There are some

interesting, old-fashioned canning techniques still in circulation but, to be sure your food is safe, use only the safest techniques available.

NOTE: According to the latest research by the U.S. Department of Agriculture, sealing jelly with paraffin is no longer recommended because jellies sealed with wax are more likely to spoil than those sealed with dome lids.

Store jams, preserves, pickles, sauces, and chutneys in a cool, dark place. For an extra measure of safety, before tasting, boil canned vegetable-based sauces for 10 minutes. Check all jars occasionally, and if you see any sign of leakage, rising bubbles, or bulging lids, throw away the contents of the jar and the lids immediately. *Do not taste— destroy it!*

Make a habit of labeling everything you make before it goes into your pantry or freezer with contents, quantity, date made, and expiration date. An expiration date on food gifts ensures that the recipient will use the food while it's at its most flavorful—and safest.

FOR JELLIES: Follow the recipes carefully, then fill the sterile jars, allowing a 1/4-inch headspace (space between the top of the jar and its contents); wipe the rims of the jars carefully with a damp towel before sealing them.

Place the hot lid on the filled jar; screw on the metal ring following manufacturer's guidelines. While still hot, place the covered jars in the rack of a hot-water bath canner. Pour in hot water to cover the jars with at least 1 inch of water. Process (boil) jellies in jars for 5 minutes. With jar lifter or long tongs, remove the jars from the hot water and set aside on a rack to cool.

As the jars cool, each lid will make a "popping" sound once. The lids will become concave, rather than bulging, and will be firm when you press on them, indicating that they are sealed. Store the jelly in a cool, dark place.

If a lid on a jar does not seal, you can either reheat the contents of the jar until boiling and repeat the sealing process with a new lid, or you can store the product in the refrigerator and use it quickly.

FOR JAMS, PRESERVES, PICKLES, SAUCES, AND CHUTNEYS: For all the processes in pickling and chutneys, use only glass, stainless steel, heavy enameled, or crockery kettles and pans; the high acid content in pickling will react with aluminum or copper. Make sure that the lids you use are approved for pickling.

Jams, preserves, pickled vegetables and fruits, sauces, and chutneys must be treated in a water bath after they are poured into clean jars and lids are in place. For a hot-water bath, place filled jars in a hot-water bath canner with a rack for holding jars. Fill the canner with hot water to cover the jars with at least 1 inch of water and bring the water to boiling. Follow processing times for the size of canning jar specified in each recipe.

Remove the jars from the hot water with tongs or jar lifter. Check the seal as indicated under "For jellies" on this page.

FOR FREEZING: Freezing is a way of preserving food that also maintains much of the food's natural qualities. Your freezer should be set for 0°F or below.

Foods that are kept frozen for longer than the recommended storage times will still be safe and usable, but the quality may not be as high.

Materials for wrapping frozen foods should be moisture- and vapor-proof and you should be able to squeeze out all the air from between the wrapper and the food.

Heavy-duty aluminum foil, plastic wrap for freezing, or laminated freezer paper can be used for wrapping bulky foods. Seal plastic and paper wraps on all sides with freezer tape.

Self-sealing freezer bags are available in quart and gallon sizes and are good containers for both solid and liquid foods. To easily fill bags with liquids, pour the liquid into a jar, cover the mouth of the jar with the bag, and carefully invert the jar so the contents go into the bag. Squeeze out the air before sealing the bag. Lay the bags flat in the freezer until solid; then you can move them around so they take less space.

Plastic and glass freezer containers are also good for liquids and juicy foods. When filling containers, remember that liquids expand when frozen, so leave a 1/2-inch to 3/4-inch headspace so the expanding food won't make the lid bulge or pop off.

MAKE A LIST AND CHECK IT TWICE

Tack a checklist inside a kitchen cupboard door to keep track of the items you've made, the date you made them, the date by which they should be used, where you've stored them, and how you plan to use them. Here's an example:

ITEM	DATE MADE	USE BY	WHERE STORED	PLANS
Mixed Herb Vinegar	9/15	one year	bottom cupboard	basket for Brent
Creole Seasoning	10/2	3/2	jar in pantry	mail to Karla
Citrus Tea Mix	10/8	3/8	jar in pantry	tree-trimming party
Brandied Jam Sauce	11/1	4/1	basement fridge	Thanksgiving dinner

■ *Strawberry Freezer Jam*

STRAWBERRY FREEZER JAM

The beauty of this jam is in its brilliant summery color as well as its fresh fruity flavor. Use only the ripest, unblemished strawberries.

4 cups strawberries, stemmed
4 cups sugar
1 teaspoon finely shredded lemon peel
2 tablespoons lemon juice
1 pouch (3 ounces) liquid pectin

Mash the strawberries in a bowl with a potato masher, then measure. There should be 2 cups. In a large bowl, stir together the berries and sugar. In a separate bowl, combine lemon peel, lemon juice, and pectin. Add to berries/sugar mixture and stir for 3 minutes. Fill clean freezer jars or containers, leaving a ½-inch headspace; cover the jars or containers and leave at room temperature for 24 hours. Refrigerate for up to 4 weeks, or freeze for up to 1 year.

Makes about 5 half-pint jars.

CALIBRATE FOR ACCURACY

To check your candy thermometer for accuracy, place the thermometer in a saucepan of boiling water for a few minutes. If it registers above or below 212°F, add or subtract the same difference in degrees from the temperature given in the recipe.

TART RED PLUM JAM

Capture the delicious tartness of red plums in glass jars. Your family will love this jam spread on hot rolls, pancakes, or peanut butter sandwiches. Also try it as a filling between layers of cake. Be sure to put aside a few jars to give as gifts.

3 pounds (about 18, 2-inch diameter) tart
red plums, washed
1¼ cups cold water
4 cups sugar

Pit and chop plums coarsely (should have 7½ cups). Put the plums and water into a large heavy pan. Bring to a boil, then reduce the heat and simmer gently, covered, for 30 minutes, or until the fruit is very tender. Remove the pan from the heat and stir in the sugar. Return to low heat and stir until the sugar is dissolved, then bring to a full boil over high heat. Boil rapidly until a candy thermometer registers 220°F. Or, remove the pan from the heat and check thickness by removing a small amount of jam with a cold metal spoon; cool slightly, then tilt. If the drops cling together in a sheet as they fall, the jam is done.

Remove the jam from the heat and let stand for 2 minutes. Skim off the foam. Stir to distribute the fruit. Ladle the jam into hot clean jars, leaving a ¼-inch headspace. Seal according to the directions on page 69, processing in boiling water for 15 minutes.

Makes about 6 half-pint jars.

QUICK CRANBERRY-APPLE JELLY

Here's a shortcut jelly that eliminates the process of cooking and juicing cranberries and apples—start with a bottle of cranberry-apple drink. The sweet/tart flavor is wonderful as a filling for Christmas cookies or melted and spread on fruitcakes as a glaze.

1 quart cranberry-apple drink
2 tablespoons lemon juice
5 cups sugar
2 pouches (3 ounces each) liquid pectin

In a large stainless steel or enameled pan, combine the cranberry-apple drink, lemon juice, and sugar. Bring to a full, rolling boil, stirring constantly. Quickly stir in the pectin. Return to a full, rolling boil and boil for 1 minute, stirring constantly. Remove from the heat and skim off the foam. Pour into hot sterile jars, leaving a ¼-inch headspace. Seal according to the directions on page 69, processing in boiling water for 5 minutes.

Makes about 6 half-pint jars.

CITRUS MARMALADE

Try this tangy, golden marmalade on buttered toast or English muffins—or spread it on crepes, roll them tightly, and top with whipped cream and a sprinkle of cinnamon.

2¼–2½ pounds (about 7 medium) fresh, unblemished oranges, scrubbed
1 lemon, scrubbed
8 cups water
8 cups sugar

Cut the oranges and lemon in half and squeeze out the juice with a reamer or in a juicer, saving the peels. Pour the juice and the water into a large stainless steel or enameled pan. Save the seeds and any pulp from the strainer or juicer and wrap them in several layers of 100% cotton cheesecloth. (The seeds and pulp contain pectin that will help the marmalade thicken.) Tie the cheesecloth closed with a long string. Chop the citrus peels into fine shreds, or chop them with the metal blade in a food processor. Add the peels and cheesecloth sack to the pan.

Bring the pan of juice and peels to a slow boil, then reduce the heat and let simmer for 1½ to 2 hours, or until the peels are very soft. Squeeze the bag well with the back of a large spoon (the bag will be very hot) and discard the bag.

Remove the pan from the heat and stir in the sugar until it is completely dissolved. Return the pan to medium-high heat and boil rapidly, without stirring, until a candy thermometer registers 220°F, about 15 to 20 minutes. Or, remove the pan from the heat and check thickness by removing a small amount of marmalade with a cold metal spoon; let it cool slightly. Tilt the spoon; if the drops cling together in a sheet as they fall, the marmalade is done. Be careful not to boil it too long or you'll have a solid mass of marmalade when it cools.

When the setting point is reached, remove from the heat and skim off the foam. Stir to evenly distribute the solids. Pour into hot clean jars, leaving a ¼-inch headspace. Seal according to the directions on page 69, processing in boiling water for 15 minutes.

Makes about 10 half-pint jars.

GINGER-LEMON JELLY

Save a jar or two of this unusual jelly for cookie-making time, when you can spread it between layers of soft ginger cookies. Your family will also enjoy this easy-to-make jelly on hot buttered biscuits and scones.

½ **cup freshly squeezed lemon juice, strained**
2 **cups water**
6 **cups sugar**
1 **tablespoon ground ginger**
2 **pouches (3 ounces each) liquid pectin**

In a large stainless steel or enameled kettle, mix the lemon juice, water, sugar, and ginger. Bring to a full, rolling boil, stirring constantly. Quickly stir in the pectin. Return to a full, rolling boil and boil for 1 minute, stirring constantly. Remove from the heat and skim off the foam. Pour into hot sterile jars, leaving a ¼-inch headspace. Seal according to the directions on page 69, processing in boiling water for 5 minutes.

Makes about 6 half-pint jars.

▪ *Quick Cranberry-Apple Jelly and Citrus Marmalade (left); Ginger-Lemon Jelly (above)*

RED AND GREEN BELL PEPPER JELLY

Once a specialty only of the Southwest, hot-pepper jelly has gained fans all over the country. The colors say "Christmas," making this jelly a natural component in Yuletide gift baskets. Serve with meat.

4–5 large green bell peppers, washed, seeded, and cored

2 large red bell peppers, washed, seeded, and cored

2 cups cider vinegar

2 teaspoons salt

2 teaspoons chili powder

10 cups sugar

$2/3$ cup lemon juice

2 pouches (3 ounces each) liquid pectin

Cut the peppers into chunks. Chop the peppers by hand or in a food processor to make 4 cups. Mix the peppers, vinegar, salt, and chili powder in a large stainless steel or enameled pan; bring to a boil and boil for 10 minutes, stirring occasionally. Add the sugar and lemon juice and return to a full, rolling boil, stirring constantly. Quickly stir in the pectin. Return to a full, rolling boil and boil for 1 minute, stirring constantly. Skim the foam from the top with a slotted spoon. Remove from the heat. Ladle the jelly into hot sterile jars, leaving a $1/4$-inch headspace. Seal according to the directions on page 69, processing in boiling water for 5 minutes.

Makes 10 to 12 half-pint jars.

▪ *Red and Green Bell Pepper Jelly (right);*
Ingredients for Spicy Apple Butter (far right)

SPICY APPLE BUTTER

Fat-free and relatively low-calorie, apple butter is a delicious spread on toast and a tasty topping or filling for yellow, applesauce, or spice cakes, or pumpkin bread.

4 pounds (about 12) cooking apples (such as Winesap or Jonathan)
2 cups apple cider or apple juice
About 4 cups brown sugar

1 teaspoon ground cinnamon
1/2 teaspoon ground cloves
1/2 teaspoon ground allspice

Wash the apples and cut out the stems and blossom ends. (Coarsely cut up the apples, if needed, to fit in the pan.) Add the apples and cider to a large pan. Cover and cook over low heat about 30 minutes, or until tender. Force the soft apples through a food mill or sieve. Discard the peels and cores. Measure the pulp and return it to the pan; add 1/2 cup sugar for each cup of pulp. Add cinnamon, cloves, and allspice. Bring to boiling; reduce heat. Simmer, uncovered, about 2 hours or until very thick, stirring often. Test for doneness by pouring a spoonful on a plate. The apple butter is done when no liquid separates from the solids. Pour hot apple butter into hot clean jars, leaving a 1/4-inch headspace. Seal according to the directions on page 69, processing in boiling water for 10 minutes.

Makes about 6 half-pint jars.

■ *English Lemon Curd*

ENGLISH LEMON CURD

Once you've discovered the fabulously lemony flavor of English Lemon Curd, you'll find many ways to enjoy it. Spread it thickly on fresh bread, muffins, scones, pound cake, or quick breads. Or, use this lemon curd to fill small tart shells or as filling between layers of sponge cake.

1 cup sugar
3 tablespoons finely shredded lemon or
   orange peel
²⁄₃ cup lemon or orange juice
3 large eggs, beaten well
½ cup (1 stick) cold unsalted butter, cut
   into small pieces

In the top of a double boiler, combine sugar, peel, juice, and eggs. Place over barely simmering water. Cook, stirring well, about 15 minutes, or until thick and smooth. Add butter pieces, a few at a time, during the last 5 minutes of cooking.

Pour into refrigerator or freezer containers. It will keep, covered, for up to 1 week in the refrigerator or 6 months in the freezer.

Makes about 2½ cups.

Preserved Fruits

Since ancient times, our foremothers knew that cooking fruit with sugar would preserve the fruit for later use. Today's methods of preserving are much the same, though we have the added benefits of screw-top lids for jars and processing that ensure a long period of safe storage.

Some of these fruit preserves are fabulous when spread on hot biscuits for breakfast or spooned onto pudding or ice cream after dinner. Others can be served as a relish with poultry or ham. Whatever their eventual use, these fruit preserves are wonderful to have on hand and to tuck into gift baskets and Christmas stockings.

Before beginning to make a recipe in this section, review "Canning Jams, Jellies, Preserves, Pickles, and Sauces" on page 68.

PRESERVED LEMONY FIGS

The sharpness of lemon offsets the sweetness of these preserved figs.

2 thin-skinned lemons
1 cup water
6 cups sugar
3 pounds (about 60) figs, washed with stems
   removed

Slice the lemons into very thin slices and remove seeds. In a large stainless steel or enameled pan, mix the water, sugar, and fruits. Cover and let stand 2 hours. Cook over medium-high heat and stir until the sugar is dissolved. Bring to a boil. Boil, uncovered,

stirring occasionally, about 5 minutes, or until the figs are clear and the syrup is thick. Stir more often as the mixture thickens to prevent scorching. Remove from the heat and let stand for 2 minutes; skim off the foam. Stir to distribute the fruit. Ladle the fruit and syrup into hot clean jars, leaving a ½-inch head-space. Seal according to the directions on page 69, processing in boiling water for 15 minutes.

Makes about 10 half-pint jars.

SUNSHINE ORANGE SLICES

These rings of orange maintain their shape and much of their color—and their flavor is intensely orange. You'll enjoy serving these unusual goodies with curries, ham, duck, and smoked poultry.

4 navel oranges with shiny, firm skins

1 tablespoon salt

¾ cup water

2 cups sugar

½ cup honey

½ cup cider vinegar

Place the oranges in a 3-quart stainless steel or enameled saucepan or 4-quart stainless steel or enameled Dutch oven in a single layer. Add enough water to cover them and add salt. Bring to a boil and boil 30 minutes. Drain. Cover the oranges with cold water and let stand 30 minutes, changing the water every 10 minutes. Drain and remove the oranges to a cutting board. Heat the oven to 325°F. In the same pan, combine the ¾ cup water with the sugar, honey, and vinegar; bring to a boil, then

lower the heat and simmer 5 minutes. Meanwhile, cut each orange into 6 thick slices and remove the seeds. Add the slices to the syrup and simmer 15 minutes. Pour into a 3-quart rectangular glass baking dish. Bake 1 hour, uncovered. Cool. Stack the slices in clean wide-mouth glasses or jars; pour the thickened syrup over top. Store in the refrigerator for up to 6 months.

Makes 2 quart jars.

▪ *Preserved Lemony Figs (left); Sunshine Orange Slices (above)*

BASKETS OF JAM TO GO

Plan the gift baskets you'll give this year so you'll be sure to have all the components on hand when gift-giving time comes. Gift baskets come in all sizes—and in all kinds of containers. Regardless of the basket's size or shape, a jar of homemade jam or marmalade is a thoughtful addition. Here are some ideas that may inspire you with combinations for gift-giving ideas:

- Line a small basket with a plaid napkin and add a jar of jam and a container of freshly made English muffins or scones in a pleasing arrangement. Insert sprigs of greens and tie a red ribbon around the basket.
- Cut five squares of lemon yellow netting large enough to line a box or basket. Offset the corners of the net squares so the corners stand out at different angles. Stuff the basket or box with a lemon-flavored quick bread, a jar of English Lemon Curd (page 77), tea bags, a small teapot, and a box of sugar cubes. Fill in spaces around the items with tiny, shiny yellow and green Christmas tree balls. Finish with a big bow made of polka dot ribbon.
- Put together an orange theme basket lined with an orange gingham kitchen towel and stuffed with Citrus Marmalade (page 72), orange muffins, and findings such as an orange mug, pencils, golf balls, etc. Wrap the basket with orange and dark green ribbons.

CORIANDER TOMATO JAM

In the mid-1950s, my mother lived in Capetown, South Africa, where, she said, the locals and visitors alike bought large cans of inexpensive—and delicious—tomato jam. While tomatoes are ripe, juicy, and plentiful, make a batch of this flavorful, deep red jam. Serve it on bagels or English muffins or with meats and cheeses.

3 pounds (about 6 large or 9 medium) fully ripe, fresh tomatoes
4 cups sugar
1/2 teaspoon ground coriander
1 package (3 ounces) lemon-flavored gelatin
2 teaspoons finely shredded lemon peel

Peel, quarter, core, and seed the tomatoes. Drain them in a colander, discarding the juice. Chop the pulp and put it in a kettle. Heat to boiling; reduce heat and simmer for 10 minutes. Measure; there should be 2½ cups. Add the sugar and coriander. Bring to boiling, stirring frequently. Remove from the heat. Add the gelatin and stir until dissolved. Stir in the lemon peel. Ladle the jam into hot clean jars or freezer containers, leaving a ½-inch headspace. Cover and label. Let stand at room temperature for several hours, or until jam is set. Store for up to 3 weeks in the refrigerator or in the freezer for up to 1 year.

Makes about 5 half-pint jars.

■ *Coriander Tomato Jam*

CHAPTER 2

Pickles and Chutneys

PICKLES ARE A PERFECT ACCOM-
PANIMENT TO THE HOLIDAY TABLE,
BUT SO MUCH MORE SPECIAL
WHEN MADE AND CANNED AT
HOME. OFFER TRADITIONAL
MOM'S BREAD-AND-BUTTER
PICKLES OR OLD-FASHIONED
GARLIC-DILL PICKLES, OR SUR-
PRISE YOUR GUESTS WITH SPICED

PICKLED PLUMS. CHUTNEYS ARE
A DELICIOUS NEW TASTE DURING
THE HOLIDAYS. IN PLACE OF
CRANBERRY, SPREAD ON HAM
AND TURKEY SANDWICHES, OR
POURED OVER CREAM CHEESE AS
AN EASY, DELECTABLE SPREAD,
YOU WILL BE AMAZED AT THE
VERSATILITY CHUTNEYS PROVIDE.

PICKLES

The preserving qualities of salt and vinegar go to work in pickling—another ancient method for keeping foods. Pickled cucumbers—with dill and garlic or with sugar and onions—are all-American favorites. Less familiar, but also delicious, are pickled plums, which add their own spicy goodness to holiday meals and gifts.

To ensure the best flavor for all pickles, use the freshest, most fragrant spices. See "Canning Jams, Jellies, Preserves, Pickles, and Sauces" on page 68 for instructions and important precautions for pickling and processing.

MOM'S BREAD-AND-BUTTER PICKLES

I was ten years old the first summer my mom made a big batch of these tasty pickles. We love them with Yankee bean soup, salty ham, or macaroni-vegetable casseroles. Use very fresh cucumbers without wax coating. Cucumbers should be picked the day you use them. Look for pickling cucumbers at farmers' markets.

4 pounds (about 16 medium or 20 small) cucumbers
3 pounds (6 to 8 large) onions
2 green bell peppers, seeded and cored
1/4 cup salt without additives or iodine
4 cups cider vinegar
4 cups sugar
2 tablespoons whole mustard seeds
2 teaspoons whole allspice
1 1/2 teaspoons whole celery seeds
1/2 teaspoon ground cloves

With a knife or in a food processor, cut the cucumbers and onions into very thin slices. Chop the peppers into about 1/2-inch pieces, or smaller if you like. Put the vegetables into a large bowl and sprinkle them with salt. Cover the vegetables with a plate and weight it with a heavy can. Refrigerate for 12 hours. Drain and rinse the vegetables in cold water. Drain thoroughly in a colander.

In a large stainless steel or enameled pan, combine the vinegar, sugar, mustard seeds, allspice, celery seeds, and cloves. Bring just to the boiling point, stirring to dissolve the sugar. Gradually add the vegetables, without stirring. Bring just to the boiling point again. Remove from the heat. With a long-handled ladle, spoon the pickles and syrup into hot clean jars, leaving a 1/2-inch headspace. Wipe the rims and seal according to the directions on page 69, processing in boiling water for 10 minutes. You can serve these pickles as soon as they're cool (but they are best served chilled).

Makes 9 pint jars.

OLD-FASHIONED GARLIC-DILL PICKLES

For best flavor, chill these crunchy pickles before serving. Use very fresh, unwaxed cucumbers.

4 pounds (about 16 medium or 20 small) cucumbers
3 cups white vinegar
3 cups water
1/4 cup salt without additives or iodine
12 cloves garlic
1/2 cup dill seeds
1 teaspoon whole black peppercorns

■ Mom's Bread-and-Butter Pickles

Cut the cucumbers in half or quarters lengthwise. If they are too long to fit into the jars, cut them in half crosswise. In a large stainless steel or enameled pan, combine the vinegar, water, salt, and garlic. Heat just to a full boil.

Pack the cucumbers into hot clean pint-size jars. To each jar, add 1 tablespoon dill seeds and a few peppercorns; divide garlic cloves among jars. Pour the hot vinegar solution over the pickles, leaving a $^1/_2$-inch headspace. Seal immediately according to the directions on page 69, processing jars in boiling water for 15 minutes.

These pickles are best if eaten after 6 weeks. Check the jars periodically and destroy any jars that have leaks or bulges or show cloudiness. Garlic may turn blue during storage, but it is harmless.

Makes about 8 pint jars.

SPICED PICKLED PLUMS

Serve these pickled plums with cold cooked meats, poultry, or cheese. They're also very good with cooked venison, pheasant, or other game.

4 cups sugar
1 $^1/_4$ cups cider or malt vinegar
4 pounds (about 25) firm, ripe plums (such as damsons, prune, or greengage)
2 tablespoons whole cloves
1 cinnamon stick (3 inches), broken
1 whole nutmeg

In a medium stainless steel or enameled pan, stir together the sugar and vinegar over low heat until the sugar has dissolved and the mixture is syrupy. Meanwhile, wash and dry the plums and remove stems. Place the plums in a very large stainless steel or enameled saucepan or Dutch oven; pour the syrup over the plums. Tie the cloves, cinnamon, and nutmeg in a 100% cotton cheesecloth bag and add to the syrup. Bring to a gentle boil and simmer for 10 minutes, covered, or until the plums are soft, but still whole. Remove cheesecloth bag. Remove the fruit with a slotted spoon and pack into hot clean jars. Pour the syrup over the fruit, leaving a $^1/_2$-inch headspace. Seal according to the directions on page 69, processing in boiling water for 20 minutes. Keep for at least 1 month before opening.

Makes 6 pint jars.

▪ *Old-Fashioned Garlic-Dill Pickles*

■ *Ingredients for Apple-Peach-Raisin Chutney*

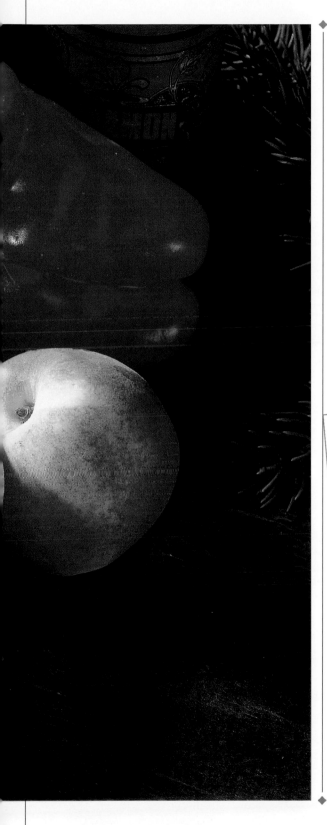

CHUTNEYS

Chutneys were "discovered" by British soldiers who were stationed in India in the nineteenth century. Nearly every meal in India is highlighted by the spicy sweetness of chutneys, which are most often made with a combination of fruits in a thick, sweet sauce. Keep a stock of chutneys to spread on turkey or ham sandwiches, to serve with curried meats or vegetables, or to give as stocking stuffers or as part of a cooking theme gift basket.

To ensure the best flavor for all chutneys, use the freshest, most fragrant spices. See "Canning Jams, Jellies, Preserves, Pickles, and Sauces" on page 68 for instructions and important precautions for processing.

STUFF A STOCKING FOR AN INDIAN FOOD LOVER

Buy or make a stocking in a rich color and lush fabric—or madras plaid. Fill it with jars of your homemade chutneys, exotic spices (cardamom, cumin, Garam Masala [page 110], and fenugreek), basmati rice, imported Indian tea, and a silver tea ball.

APPLE-PEACH-RAISIN CHUTNEY

A must with curries, this sweet and spicy chutney can also be spread on turkey or ham sandwiches or mixed into mayonnaise for a salad dressing or dip. To make preparation extra-easy, whirl the fruits and vegetables in a food processor. If you prefer, you can use only apples or peaches, instead of the combination of both.

4 cups (about 2 pounds) peeled, cored, and coarsely chopped apples
4 cups (about 2 pounds) peeled, pitted, and coarsely chopped peaches
1 cup chopped onions
1 cup chopped red bell peppers
2 cloves garlic, minced
1 pound dark raisins
2⅓ cups (1 pound) dark brown sugar
2 cups cider vinegar
1 tablespoon ground ginger
1 tablespoon ground cinnamon
2 teaspoons dry mustard
2 teaspoons salt
½ teaspoon dried, crushed red chili peppers (or to taste)

Stir all ingredients together in a very large stainless steel or enameled kettle. Slowly bring to a boil and, stirring occasionally, boil gently for about 45 to 60 minutes, or until thick. (Stir more often toward the end of cooking time to prevent scorching.)

While still boiling hot, ladle chutney into hot clean jars, leaving a ¼-inch headspace. Seal according to the directions on page 69, processing in boiling water for 10 minutes. Store for at least 1 month before serving.

Makes 8 half-pint jars.

GOLDEN PINEAPPLE CHUTNEY

Light in color and delightfully spicy, this chutney is terrific served with bean soup, stews, and any meat or poultry. During preparation, wear thin rubber gloves to protect your hands from the red peppers—and be careful not to touch your face!

4 to 8 small, dried red chili peppers
¼ cup cold water
3 cans (20 ounces each) pineapple tidbits or chunks*(juice pack) (about 7 cups)
3 cups white vinegar
2 cups firmly packed light brown sugar
1 teaspoon salt
1 cup golden raisins
2 tablespoons chopped crystallized ginger
3 cloves garlic, minced

Soak the peppers in the water for 30 minutes. Drain. Remove and discard seeds and finely chop the peppers. In a large stainless steel or enameled kettle, add the pineapple (with juice), vinegar, sugar, salt, raisins, ginger, and garlic. Bring to a boil; reduce heat and simmer, uncovered, for 45 minutes, stirring occasionally, until thickened. (Stir more often toward the end of cooking time to prevent scorching.)

Ladle the hot chutney into hot clean jars, leaving a ¼-inch headspace. Seal according to the directions on page 69, processing in boiling water for 10 minutes. Store for at least 1 week before serving.

Makes 6 half-pint jars.

*If using chunks, drain juice into a bowl and chop the pineapple into small pieces.

▪ *Golden Pineapple Chutney*

PENNSYLVANIA DUTCH CORN RELISH

This sweet-and-sour relish is great on hot dogs or served with corned beef, ham, or scrambled eggs. Use your food processor for faster preparation. It's important to use the measured amounts.

About 5 cups yellow corn kernels (cut from 10 ears of fresh corn)
1½ cups (about 2 medium) green bell peppers, chopped
1½ cups (about 2 medium) red bell peppers, chopped
2 cups (about 2 large) yellow onions, chopped
4 cups (about 1 small head) green cabbage, cored and chopped or shredded
2¼ cups sugar
1 tablespoon dry mustard
1 tablespoon celery seeds
1 tablespoon salt
1 tablespoon turmeric
2¾ cups cider vinegar
½ cup water

Place all ingredients in a large stainless steel or enameled kettle. Bring to a boil and simmer, covered, for 30 minutes, or until the vegetables are tender. Ladle into hot clean jars, leaving a ½-inch headspace. Seal according to the directions on page 69, processing in boiling water for 15 minutes. Store for at least 1 month before serving.

Makes 5 pint jars.

■ *Pennsylvania Dutch Corn Relish*

Sauces—Savory and Sweet

SAUCES, ESPECIALLY THOSE MADE AHEAD OF TIME, ARE A LIFESAVER DURING BUSY HOLIDAY ENTERTAINING. SAVORY SAUCES ARE GREAT TOSSED OVER PASTA FOR AN EASY MEAL, ACCENTING EGGS FOR A FAMILY

BREAKFAST, OR AVAILABLE FOR DIPPING WITH A VARIETY OF HORS D'OEUVRES. SWEET SAUCES MAKE DESSERTS A SNAP. POURED OVER ICE CREAM, POUND CAKE, CHEESECAKE— THE POSSIBILITIES ARE ENDLESS.

■ *Texas Chili Sauce*

Savory Sauces

Give family meals a perk or save pretty jars of these sauces to give to friends. Before the first freeze, while tomatoes are juicy and ripe, make Texas Chili Sauce (below) and Chunky Pasta Sauce (right). A variety of flavored mustards and soy sauce–based dipping sauces can be made and enjoyed any time of year.

Before beginning to make any recipe in this section, read "Canning Jams, Jellies, Preserves, Pickles, and Sauces" on page 68.

TEXAS CHILI SAUCE

You'll be glad you have plenty of this pleasantly spicy chili sauce in your pantry to use on scrambled eggs, macaroni and cheese, chicken enchiladas, and spinach soufflé.

8 pounds (about 16 large) ripe, unblemished
    tomatoes
2 onions, chopped
1 cup sugar
1 cup vinegar
4 teaspoons salt
1 teaspoon ground cinnamon
1 teaspoon dry mustard
1 teaspoon curry powder
1/2 teaspoon ground nutmeg
1/2 teaspoon ground red pepper (or to taste)

Core and cut up the tomatoes (should have 16 cups). Place tomatoes and onions in an 8-to 10-quart stainless steel or enameled pan; bring to a boil over medium heat, stirring occasionally. Reduce the heat and cook, uncovered, for 10 to 15 minutes, or until the vegetables are soft. Using a food mill or a wooden spoon and a colander, press the tomato mixture to remove the skins and seeds (should have about 12 cups of mixture). Return to the pan and add the sugar, vinegar, salt, cinnamon, mustard, curry powder, nutmeg, and pepper. Bring to a boil. Boil gently, uncovered, for 1 1/2 hours, or until thickened. Pour into hot clean jars, leaving a 1/2-inch headspace. Seal according to the directions on page 69, processing in boiling water for 15 minutes.

Makes about 6 half-pint jars.

CHUNKY PASTA SAUCE

Go ahead and make a big batch of this versatile tomato sauce. Let it cool, then pour in one- or two-cup portions into self-sealing freezer bags. Squeeze out the air before sealing them. Lay the bags flat in the freezer until frozen solid; then you can move them around. Thaw the sauce in the refrigerator or quickly in the microwave before heating and using on pasta, squash, or eggplant, or in casseroles.

1/2 cup olive oil
2 cups finely chopped carrots
2 cups finely chopped onions
1 cup finely chopped celery (including
    leaves)
6 cloves garlic, finely minced
10 pounds (about 20 large) tomatoes, peeled,
    seeded, and chopped (about 12 cups)
4 bay leaves
2 teaspoons dried oregano, crushed, or 2
    tablespoons snipped, fresh
About 1 tablespoon salt
About 1 1/2 teaspoons pepper

In a large Dutch oven, heat the oil. Add the carrots, onions, celery, and garlic; cook about 5 minutes, or until the vegetables are tender but not brown. Add the tomatoes, bay leaves, and oregano. Bring to boiling, reduce heat, and simmer, uncovered, about 45 to 60 minutes, or until thickened. Add salt and pepper, and adjust seasoning to taste. Remove bay leaves and store in the refrigerator for up to 3 days or in the freezer for up to 1 year.

Makes about 2 1/2 quarts.

CHINESE DIPPING SAUCE

Sweet, sour, and salty, this thin sauce is very good with Chinese dumplings, spareribs, and egg rolls or brushed on grilled pork, lamb, shrimp, or chicken.

1 cup firmly packed dark brown sugar
1/4 cup cider vinegar
1/4 cup soy sauce
1 teaspoon ground ginger
1/4 teaspoon garlic powder

Mix together all ingredients until the sugar dissolves. Use immediately or refrigerate for up to 6 months. Stir before using.

Makes 1 1/2 cups.

▪ *Chunky Pasta Sauce (left); Chinese Dipping Sauce (right); Spicy Sweet 'n' Sour Sauce (far right)*

SPICY SWEET 'N' SOUR SAUCE

Try this quick-mix sauce for dipping fried shrimp or chicken nuggets. Or, roll cooked meatballs in the sauce and serve them from a chafing dish as hot hors d'oeuvres. Mix a bit into turkey salad or spread it on ham sandwiches. Your guests will never guess how simple this sauce is.

1 jar (18 ounces) orange marmalade
3 tablespoons brown mustard
1 tablespoon prepared horseradish

In a medium bowl, combine all the ingredients. Pack in clean jars or plastic containers and cover well. Store in the refrigerator for up to 3 months or in the freezer for up to 6 months.

Makes about 2 cups.

HOMEMADE MUSTARD

When mustard powder is first mixed with water, it is hot stuff! But don't be alarmed—it loses most of its fire as it "ripens." Make a variety of flavored mustards, pack them in small jars, and give variety packs to co-workers and neighbors during the holidays. Try adding 1 tablespoon Homemade Mustard to ¼ cup mayonnaise or salad dressing for a sandwich spread.

½ cup dry mustard
1 teaspoon sugar
¼ teaspoon salt
1 teaspoon cider vinegar
2 tablespoons cooking oil
⅓ cup cold water

In a small saucepan, mix the mustard, sugar, and salt. Gradually add the vinegar, oil, and water, beating with a whisk until smooth. Heat to boiling. Cool slightly. Spoon into a clean jar, cover, and refrigerate. Mustard will keep almost indefinitely in the refrigerator. If the mustard is too thick, add water to get the consistency you desire.

Makes ½ cup.

VARIATION: Before chilling, add 1½ teaspoons minced fresh dillweed, 1 tablespoon honey, or 1 tablespoon prepared horseradish. If the mustard is too thick, add water to get the consistency you desire.

▪ *Homemade Mustards*

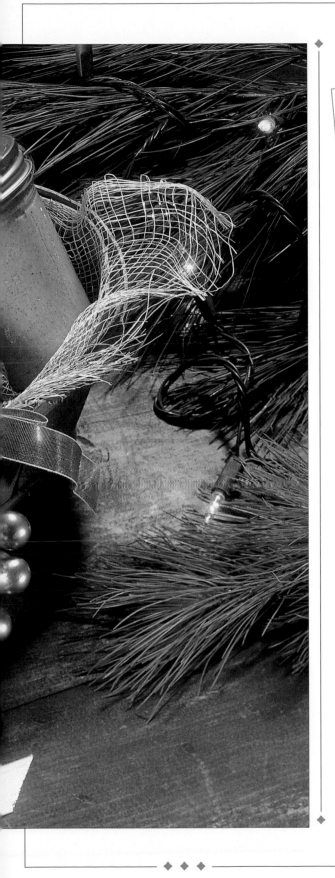

TASTY BUTTERS

You can give meals, sandwiches, and snacks an extra zing with flavored butters. Pack the butters in small, straight-sided bowls (such as soufflé cups), cover them with rounds of waxed paper, and refrigerate for up to one week. For longer storage, form the soft butter into slabs, chill until solid, place in self-sealing freezer bags, and freeze for up to three months. To serve, thaw in the refrigerator, then soften and pack in bowls or melt to pour over hot foods.

HERB BUTTER (*serve on popcorn, steaks, lamb chops, fish, or vegetables*). Cream 1/2 cup softened butter with any of the following: 2 tablespoons minced chives; 3 tablespoons finely snipped fresh dillweed and 1/8 teaspoon ground nutmeg; 2 tablespoons minced parsley and 2 tablespoons lemon juice; or 1 tablespoon finely snipped fresh tarragon and 2 teaspoons white wine vinegar.

WATERCRESS BUTTER (*serve with seafood, chicken, or vegetables, or spread on egg salad sandwiches*). Cream 1/2 cup softened butter with 1/4 cup finely snipped watercress leaves and a dash of pepper.

LEMON-PEPPER BUTTER (*serve with seafood, poultry, or broccoli, or spread on hot Italian bread*). Cream 1/2 cup softened butter with 1 tablespoon lemon juice, 1 teaspoon finely shredded lemon peel, and 1/2 teaspoon freshly ground black pepper.

ORANGE BUTTER (*serve with hot cooked carrots, parsnips, brussels sprouts, acorn squash, or beets*). Cream 1/2 cup softened butter with 1 tablespoon finely shredded orange peel. Let stand at least one hour before using.

Sweet Sauces

A special, homemade sauce can transform a nice dessert into a sensational sweet. Creamy or fruity sauces are delicious on toasted pound-cake slices, ice cream, cheesecake, or sweet filled crepes. Make a batch of sauces now to have on hand to delight your family and guests.

If you plan to give any of these sauces as gifts, put them in jars or plastic containers. Make labels that include ways the sauces can be served, how to store them, and expiration dates. Paste or tie the labels onto the containers.

HOT FUDGE SAUCE

Try this semi-sweet chocolate sauce as a fondue for dipping strawberries, bananas, dried fruit, and sponge cake. For another quick, sensational dessert, pour enough fudge sauce in a prepared graham cracker pie shell to cover the bottom. Place in freezer until sauce is set. Fill the shell with softened ice cream and freeze until hard. Serve drizzled with more Hot Fudge Sauce.

6 ounces unsweetened chocolate, coarsely chopped
$1/4$ cup butter
2 cups sugar
1 cup half-and-half or light cream
1 can (14 ounces) sweetened condensed milk

In a 2-quart saucepan, melt the chocolate and butter over low heat, stirring constantly. Add the sugar and cream. Stir in the milk. Bring just to boiling, stirring constantly. Serve immediately or cool and store in the refrigerator in a covered container for up to 2 weeks or in the freezer for up to 6 months.

To reheat: Place the opened jar in a microwave and heat on high for 1 minute. Stir and heat for 30 seconds more. Test temperature and continue to stir and heat at 15-second intervals until warm. Or, place the sauce in a saucepan and heat, stirring, over low heat until warm.

Makes about 4 cups.

VARIATIONS: For peanut butter–fudge sauce, stir in $1/2$ cup smooth peanut butter with the milk. For mocha-fudge sauce, dissolve 2 tablespoons instant coffee crystals in 1 tablespoon hot water. Add with the milk.

TOFFEE SAUCE

Top warm waffles with scoops of vanilla ice cream, then pour on the Toffee Sauce and sprinkle with toasted chopped pecans for a scrumptious dessert.

$1^1/2$ cups sugar
1 cup evaporated milk
4 tablespoons butter
$1/4$ cup light corn syrup
1 cup crushed chocolate-covered toffee candy bars

In a medium saucepan, heat sugar, milk, butter, and corn syrup to boiling, stirring constantly. Continue stirring and boil for 1 minute. Remove from the heat and stir in the candy. Serve immediately or cool and store in a covered container in the refrigerator for up to 1 week or in the freezer for up to 6 months. Reheat to serve.

Makes $2^1/2$ cups.

BRANDIED JAM SAUCE

Any of the flavor variations on this simple theme go very well with bread pudding, rice pudding, pound cake, or chocolate cake. If you like more or less of a brandy flavor, adjust the water and brandy ratio to your liking.

2 jars (10 to 12 ounces each) jam or preserves (apricot, peach, pineapple, plum, raspberry, or strawberry)
$1/4$ cup water
$1/4$ cup brandy

Combine the jam or preserves and water in a small saucepan. Bring to a boil. Stir in the brandy and return just to boiling. Serve immediately or store in a covered container in the refrigerator for up to 6 months.

Makes about $2^1/4$ cups.

PINEAPPLE TOPPING

You can make this topping any time of year with products from your pantry shelf. For a special Christmas topping, stir in some chopped green candied or green maraschino cherries just before serving. It's terrific on ice cream, cheesecake, pound cake, or waffles.

$3^1/2$ cups sugar
1 can (20 ounces) crushed pineapple
$1/4$ cup coarsely chopped red maraschino cherries
$3/4$ cup water
2 pouches (3 ounces each) liquid pectin

Measure the sugar and set aside. In a Dutch oven, mix pineapple (with juice), cherries, and water. Add the sugar and mix well. Bring to a full, rolling boil, stirring constantly. Quickly stir in the pectin. Return to a full, rolling boil and boil for 1 minute, stirring constantly. Remove from the heat. Stir and skim off the foam for 5 minutes. Pour the topping into hot clean jars, leaving a $1/4$-inch headspace. Seal according to the directions on page 69, processing in boiling water for 15 minutes.

Makes about 5 half-pint jars.

▪ *Clockwise from left: Pineapple Topping; Toffee Sauce; Hot Fudge Sauce*

Flavor Mixes

WHEN PLANNING BIG, COMPLI-
CATED HOLIDAY MEALS, YOU
WANT TO HAVE A FEW TRUSTY
FLAVORS TO FALL BACK ON. AND
YOU WANT THE FLAVORS YOU USE
TO HAVE THE FRESHEST TASTE

POSSIBLE. HERE ARE NUMEROUS
IDEAS FOR PRESERVING SUMMER
FLAVORS—IN RICE MIX, PESTO,
VINEGARS, AND HANDY SPICE
BLENDS—SO GREAT TASTES ARE
ALWAYS AT YOUR FINGERTIPS.

Herbs For Flavor

The heady aromas and flavors of fresh herbs are at their height in late summer and early fall. Unfortunately, there's no way to preserve all the sensation of freshly picked herbs, but we can tuck away bits of the best flavors of summer to last throughout the year. Gather up an armful of fresh herbs—from your garden or supermarket—and stock your freezer and pantry with handy, flavorful mixtures.

PESTO

Traditionally, pesto is made by crushing fresh herbs in a mortar with a heavy pestle—a long and tedious job. Today, a whirl in a blender or food processor makes pesto the quick and easy way. Add fresh or thawed pesto dollops to pasta, meat loaf, or bread recipes.

2 cups firmly packed fresh basil leaves
¾ cup olive oil
½ cup grated Parmesan cheese
½ cup lightly packed fresh flat-leaf parsley sprigs
¼ cup pine nuts or walnuts
2 cloves garlic, quartered

Place all ingredients in a food processor bowl with a metal blade or in a blender. Cover and process or blend until the mixture is finely chopped, but not pureed, stopping to scrape the sides as necessary. To refrigerate, spoon pesto into a container and pour a thin coat of oil (about 1 tablespoon) on the surface to prevent darkening. Cover and refrigerate at least 2 hours to blend flavors. Keeps for up to 1 week.

To freeze: Cover a cookie sheet with plastic wrap. Drop pesto by tablespoons onto the plastic wrap. Cover lightly with another sheet of plastic wrap. Freeze until firm, about 2 hours. Remove pesto dollops to a self-sealing freezer bag or container. Freeze for up to 6 months.

Makes 1 1/4 cups.

VARIATION: Substitute fresh spinach leaves for the basil and add 2 teaspoons dried basil, crushed.

HERBED FLOUR

Keep a jar of this seasoned flour on hand to coat chicken or fish, or use it in bread, biscuit, or muffin recipes, substituting it for up to half the flour called for in recipes.

2 cups all-purpose flour
2 tablespoons dried herbs (combination of basil, dill, oregano, tarragon, and/or thyme), crushed
1/2 teaspoon black or white pepper

Combine all ingredients in a jar or refrigerator container. Cover tightly. Keeps for up to 1 year in the refrigerator or freezer.

Makes 2 cups.

▪ *Pesto (left); Herbed Rice Mix (right)*

HERBED RICE MIX

Serve the cooked rice with lightly seasoned grilled, broiled, or sautéed meat or poultry. To make larger quantities, double or triple all ingredients, and divide evenly among containers.

1 cup long-grain white or brown rice
1/4 cup chopped dried mushrooms and/or snipped dried tomatoes (not oil-packed)
1 tablespoon minced dried onions
2 teaspoons dried parsley flakes
2 teaspoons instant chicken bouillon granules
1/2 teaspoon dried oregano or thyme, crushed
1 bay leaf

Combine all ingredients in a tightly covered container. Store in cool, dry place for up to 6 months.

Makes 1 1/3 cups rice mix.

To cook: Bring 2 1/2 cups water to boiling in a medium saucepan. Add 1 1/3 cups rice mix. Bring to boiling. Reduce heat; simmer, covered, about 15 minutes for white rice (35 minutes for brown rice), or until the rice is tender and the water is absorbed. Remove bay leaf.

Makes 3 cups cooked rice.

HERBED SUGAR

Sprinkle this flavorful sugar on cookies, cakes, muffins, or fruit salads—or mix it into lemonade or tea.

2 or 3 sprigs fresh herbs (mint, lavender, or lemon thyme)
2 cups sugar

Wash herbs. Dry thoroughly with paper towels. Fill a jar one-third full with sugar. Add the herbs, then fill the jar with the remaining sugar. Leave for 2 to 3 weeks, then remove the herbs. If the sugar cakes, it may be necessary to break it up before using.

Makes 2 cups.

MEADOW MINT CONCENTRATE FOR BEVERAGES

Enjoy the essence of fresh mint any time of the year by freezing this concentrate in ice cube trays, then transferring the frozen cubes to freezer bags for easy storage. The frozen cubes can be used to flavor iced tea. Just put the frozen cubes in tall glasses and pour cold or hot tea over them. Or, for other mint-flavored beverages, melt the cubes and pour the liquid over crushed ice; or mix with ginger ale or lemon-lime soda. You can also drink the Meadow Mint Concentrate hot. Melt the frozen cubes in a mug in the microwave or in a saucepan on the stovetop. Serve in mugs and float half a lemon slice in the beverage.

2 cups firmly packed fresh mint leaves
2 lemons, sliced and seeded
1 cup sugar
2 quarts boiling water

Put the mint leaves in a very large bowl. Add the lemon slices and sugar. Pour the water into the bowl. Stir to dissolve the sugar. Cover loosely and let stand overnight. Strain through a fine sieve and discard the solids. Store in a jar or container in the refrigerator for up to 1 week or freeze in ice cube trays, then transfer cubes to plastic freezer bags and store in the freezer for up to 6 months.

Makes 2 quarts.

■ *Hot beverage made from Meadow Mint Concentrate (left); Salt-Free All-Purpose Seasoning (above)*

SALT-FREE ALL-PURPOSE SEASONING

Perfect for people on low-salt diets, this seasoning mix can be used as a salt substitute for preparing vegetables, salads, breads, fish, or poultry.

2 tablespoons dried dillweed
2 tablespoons toasted sesame seeds
2 tablespoons onion powder
1 teaspoon dried thyme, crushed
1 teaspoon celery seeds
1/2 teaspoon garlic powder
1/2 teaspoon paprika
1/8 teaspoon pepper

Combine all the ingredients in a small bowl. Store in a small, covered canister or shaker. Stir before using.

Makes about 1/3 cup.

Flavored Vinegars

Among the simplest to make, yet most impressive gifts, flavored vinegars are very useful for making dressings and marinades, while preserving some of that wonderful aroma of summer. Be very sure the vinegar you begin with has at least 4% to 6% acid content, to ensure that the vinegar will preserve the herbs. Do not dilute vinegar with water before adding the herbs. Store vinegar only in glass, plastic, or stainless steel containers with noncorrosive lids or corks.

MIXED HERB VINEGAR

This is a quantity recipe to make ahead for gift-giving time. See page 138 for an idea for sealing your gift bottles of vinegar for spectacular presentation. If you like the look of herbs floating in bottles of vinegar, add clean, fresh herbs to the bottles before sealing.

8 shallots, peeled and bruised
8 tarragon stalks (6 inches each)
8 rosemary stalks (6 inches each)
4 sprigs flat-leaf parsley
4 slices (¼-inch thick) peeled fresh ginger root
2 tablespoons sugar or honey
1 tablespoon whole black peppercorns
1 gallon vinegar (white, red, cider, malt, or
   wine, with 4% to 6% acid content)

Put all the ingredients into a gallon crock or jar. (If you don't have a gallon container, you can divide the ingredients among four 1-quart jars.) Cover and store in a cool, dark place for 2 to 3 weeks. Strain the vinegar, discard the herbs and spices, and pour the vinegar into clean wine or decorative bottles. (Use corks or nonmetal caps.) Keeps for up to 1 year.

Makes 1 gallon.

DRYING HERBS

You can dry and keep your homegrown or purchased fresh herbs for up to a year. First, remove any wilted or dead leaves from the stalks of herbs. Tie bunches of herbs together at the stalk end and carefully put each bunch, leaf-end first, into a paper bag—not plastic. Loosely tie the bag closed. Hang the bag in a dry place with a temperature of 70° to 90°F. Leave for two weeks, then remove the herbs from the bags and check for dryness. (If the herbs are not completely dry, they will mold when stored.) Never put herbs in the microwave to dry because they may ignite. But if you want to make sure they are dry, place them in a 100°F oven for 10 minutes. Strip the dry leaves off the stalks and store, covered, in glass or plastic jars away from heat and light.

Check the piquancy of dry herbs every month or so by sniffing quickly. If you can't identify the herb immediately, the herb is past its prime.

Dried herbs have more seasoning strength than fresh herbs. Use about one-third the amount of dried herbs as fresh herbs called for in recipes.

▪ *Basil Vinegar (left); Mixed Herb Vinegar (right)*

BASIL VINEGAR

Capture the flavor of basil—lemon basil, cinnamon basil, or anise basil are all excellent choices—in this simple mixture. A tinge of color as well as the flavor of the herb is infused in this vinegar.

8 cups lightly packed basil leaves
1 gallon white vinegar (4% to 6% acid content)

Put the basil in a 1-gallon glass or plastic jar. Pour the vinegar over the basil. Cover the jar with a noncorrosive lid or plastic wrap, then a tight-fitting lid. Leave in a cool, dark place for 1 month. Strain the vinegar and pour it into clean wine or decorative bottles. (Use corks or nonmetal caps.) Keeps up to 1 year.

Makes 1 gallon.

FROZEN CONVENIENCE

Gather fresh herbs to freeze for the future. Chop or snip fresh herbs, such as dill, basil, parsley, chives, or tarragon, and put one-tablespoon portions into ice cube trays. Fill with water and freeze solid. Remove the frozen herb cubes from the ice cube trays, place in a large freezer bag, and label.

To use the herbs, drop the cubes into soups, stews, or stocks. Or, thaw the cubes in a strainer, then use the herbs as you would fresh herbs. (You can save the herb-flavored water to use.) Frozen herbs have nearly the same flavoring power as fresh herbs, so use equal amounts called for in recipes.

Spice Blends

Ideal as stocking stuffers or tucked into gift baskets, customized spice blends are easy to make and fun to receive. Mix spices to flavor beef, poultry, vegetables, or pies. Be sure to include a handwritten recipe card with suggestions for ways the recipient can use the spice blend.

Spices and dried herbs stored at room temperature are best used within six months and should be replaced after a year. Store in a cool, dark place; they will keep freshest in the refrigerator or freezer.

CREOLE SEASONING

Rub this spicy-hot seasoning on beef, pork, or chicken before grilling, or add a pinch or two to a Western omelet or to flavor your own fresh salsa.

2 tablespoons paprika
1 tablespoon dried thyme, crushed
2 teaspoons onion powder
2 teaspoons garlic powder
2 teaspoons salt
2 teaspoons firmly packed brown sugar
2 teaspoons freshly ground black pepper
1 teaspoon ground red pepper
1 teaspoon ground white pepper

Mix all ingredients in a small bowl. Store in a covered jar or self-sealing plastic bag in a cool, dark place for up to 6 months.

Makes about ⅓ cup.

GARAM MASALA

Garam Masala is a complex blend of flavors and is good used in place of curry powder in lamb, chicken, pork, beef, or mixed vegetable curries. If you don't care for hot spices, omit the crushed red pepper. Whole exotic spices are available from specialty shops and by mail order.

2 tablespoons whole cumin seeds
1 tablespoon whole coriander seeds
1 tablespoon whole fenugreek
1 tablespoon black peppercorns
2 teaspoons whole mustard seeds
1 tablespoon crushed red pepper
1 tablespoon ground cinnamon
1 tablespoon poppy seeds
2 teaspoons cardamom seeds
2 teaspoons ground ginger
1½ teaspoons ground turmeric

Heat a medium-size heavy skillet over medium-low heat just until the skillet is hot. Add the cumin seeds, coriander seeds, fenugreek, peppercorns, and mustard seeds. Stirring constantly to prevent burning, heat the spices for 5 minutes. Remove from the heat and let cool. Add red pepper, cinnamon, poppy seeds, cardamom seeds, ginger, and turmeric. Grind all ingredients together in a blender or spice mill. Store in a tightly covered container in a cool, dry place for up to 6 months or in the freezer for up to 1 year.

Makes ¾ cup.

Spice Blends

ARIZONA CHILI POWDER

Mexican food lovers will find many ways to incorporate this spice mixture in guacamole, tortilla soup, enchilada sauce, and refried beans.

1/4 cup paprika
1 tablespoon ground turmeric
1 tablespoon ground cumin
2 teaspoons garlic salt
1 teaspoon dried oregano
1/2 teaspoon ground red pepper (or to taste)

Mix all ingredients in a small bowl. Store in a covered jar or plastic container in the refrigerator or freezer for up to 6 months.

Makes 1/2 cup.

HERB MIX FOR SOUP OR STOCK

When you give these little bags as gifts, include your favorite soup recipe and make a note on the instruction tag that the cook may tie a sprig of fresh parsley onto the bag before dropping it into the simmering liquid. Use one bag of herb mix with each 4 to 5 cups of chicken or turkey broth. This herb mix is especially good in chicken or turkey stocks and bean soup. You may wish to include two bags of herb mix with a jar of Eight-Bean Soup Mix (page 129) as a gift.

2 bay leaves, broken in half
2 squares dried lemon peel*
1 teaspoon dried thyme
1 teaspoon dried tarragon

Place all the ingredients in a pile in the center of a 4-inch square double thickness of 100% cotton cheesecloth. Bring all the corners to the center and tie securely with kitchen string. Leave a 6-inch tail of string so parsley can be added. Store in a cool, dry place. The herb bag should be immersed in the stock or soup during the last 10 to 20 minutes of cooking, then discarded.

Makes 1 herb bag; enough to season 4 to 5 cups of stock.

*To dry lemon peel, cut peel from a lemon into 1-inch squares and place between layers of paper towels. Store in a cool, dry place for 24 hours.

◆ *Herb Mix for Soup or Stock (above); Ginger-Loaded Apple Pie Spice (right)*

GINGER-LOADED APPLE PIE SPICE

This apple pie spice mix is complete—except for the apples. To use the mix: Peel, core, and slice five or six baking apples. Spread one-third of the apple slices in a pastry-lined 9-inch pie plate; then sprinkle with 3 table-spoons Ginger Loaded Apple Pie Spice; repeat the layers twice. Dot the apples with 1 table-spoon butter, and top with a pricked crust. Bake at 375°F for 45 to 50 minutes.

1 3/4 cups granulated sugar or firmly packed brown sugar
1/4 cup all-purpose flour
2 tablespoons finely minced crystallized ginger
1 teaspoon ground ginger
1 teaspoon ground cinnamon
1/2 teaspoon ground nutmeg

Mix all the ingredients in a medium bowl. Store in a covered jar, plastic container, or self-sealing freezer bag in the freezer for up to 1 year.

Makes 2¼ cups; enough for 4 pies.

VARIATION: Use the same seasoning mix for pear pie by substituting 5 large ripe but firm pears, which have been peeled, cored, and sliced, instead of the apples.

If you don't care for ginger, simply omit the crystallized and ground ginger.

SPICE MIX FOR MULLED WINE OR CIDER

Fill a gift basket with this fragrant spice mixture, along with the recipe and bottles of wine or cider for making the beverages, and take it as a special "Merry Christmas" to a favorite neighbor, teacher, doctor, or anyone else you'd like to remember with a gift during the holidays.

SPICE MIX:
Dried peel of 1 orange*
Dried peel of 1 lemon*
2 cinnamon sticks (2 inches each)
1 teaspoon cardamom seeds
6 whole cloves
6 whole allspice
1 whole nutmeg, crushed**

FOR MULLED WINE:
2 bottles (750ml each) red wine
½ cup creme de cassis
Cinnamon sticks (optional)

FOR MULLED CIDER:
1½ quarts apple cider
2 cups cranberry juice cocktail
Cinnamon sticks (optional)

Place all the spice mix ingredients in a 10-inch square double thickness of 100% cotton cheesecloth. Bring all four corners of the cheesecloth to the center and tie securely with kitchen string or heavy thread. Store the spice bag in a covered jar or plastic container in the refrigerator for up to 2 months or in the freezer for up to 6 months.

To make the mulled wine or cider: In a large stainless steel or heat-proof ceramic pan, bring the wine and cassis or the cider and cranberry juice just to the boiling point.

Reduce the heat to a slow simmer and add the bag of spices. Simmer, covered, for 30 minutes, then remove spice bag. Ladle into cups or mugs and serve each garnished with a cinnamon stick, if using.

Makes 8 to 10 servings.

*To dry orange and lemon peel: Wash fruit well and peel with a vegetable peeler or small, sharp knife very carefully to avoid cutting into the white pith. Peel in one continuous spiral, if possible. Dry between 2 paper towels on wire racks at room temperature for 1 to 3 days, or until the peel is dry but still pliable.

**To crush nutmeg, place it in a small self-sealing bag. Hit gently with the flat side of a meat mallet or hammer.

■ *Mulled Wine*

WRAP IT UP

Pour your spice blends into freezer bags and seal. Store the labeled bags in the refrigerator or freezer until you're ready to use them or give them away.

If you're giving the spice blend as a gift, make a decorative bag by cutting a rectangle of fabric twice the size of the freezer bag. Fold the fabric in half crosswise, then sew the two long sides of the fabric closed to make a bag. Or, you can leave three sides open and simply fold over the fabric and tie the top closed with ribbon.

- For a rustic, country look, use muslin, gingham, or calico for the fabric bag and tie the bag with raffia, rickrack, straw, or rough string.
- To present Indian spice blends, make the bag out of a brightly printed fabric and tie it with metallic gold ribbon.
- For a Victorian presentation, make the bags with velvet, brocade, or lace and tie them with layers of gorgeous shiny or lacy ribbons.

Homemade Mixes

THESE MIXES COMBINE THE CONVENIENCE OF PACKAGED MIXES WITH THE GOODNESS OF HOMEMADE. HAVING A BEVY OF THESE MIXES IN YOUR PANTRY FOR BAKING AND COOKING AND FOR BEVERAGES IS A BLESSING ON THOSE DAYS WHEN YOU DON'T HAVE TIME TO COOK. WHILE YOU'RE ENJOYING THE CONVENIENCE OF THESE

DELICIOUS MIXES, REMEMBER TO SHARE THEM WITH YOUR FRIENDS DURING THE HOLIDAYS. AN ATTRACTIVE JAR FILLED WITH A MIX FOR OATMEAL COOKIES OR WHOLE-WHEAT CORNBREAD—AND A CARD WITH INSTRUCTIONS FOR USING THE MIX—IS ALWAYS APPRECI-ATED BY PEOPLE WHO ARE HARRIED DURING THE HOLIDAYS.

VERSATILE BAKING MIX

This baking mix has everything going for it—it's inexpensive, easy to make, and very handy. On the pages following the master recipe, you'll find several suggestions for using the mix. It keeps well for six weeks at room temperature or six months in the freezer, so if you plan to do a lot of baking and cooking, double the recipe and store this tasty mix in gallon-size jars.

10 cups (2½ pounds) all-purpose flour
2 cups nonfat dry milk powder
⅓ cup baking powder
¼ cup sugar
1 tablespoon salt
1½ teaspoons cream of tartar
2 cups (1 pound) shortening (that does not require refrigeration)

In a very large bowl, thoroughly stir together the flour, dry milk, baking powder, sugar, salt, and cream of tartar. With a pastry blender, cut in the shortening until the mixture resembles corn meal. Store in a tightly covered container at room temperature for up to 6 weeks or for up to 6 months in the freezer. To use, pile the mix lightly in a measuring cup and level with a spatula or knife.

Makes 15 cups.

▪ *Pancakes made with Versatile Baking Mix*

Recipes for using Versatile Baking Mix:

PANCAKES

This recipe can be doubled or tripled. If you have pancakes leftover from breakfast, serve them later in the day—spread with peanut butter and jelly or cream cheese. Or, wrap them well and freeze them for up to one month. Reheat in the microwave or on a hot griddle.

About ¾ cup water
1 egg
1½ cups Versatile Baking Mix

In a medium bowl, mix together the ¾ cup water and egg. (If you like thinner pancakes, add 2 tablespoons more water.) Lightly stir in baking mix, just until dry ingredients are moistened. Pour ¼-cup portions onto a hot, lightly greased griddle or skillet. When the top is blistered with bubbles, flip the pancakes over and cook until the undersides are brown. Serve hot with butter and honey, syrup, Spicy Apple Butter (page 75), or Strawberry Freezer Jam (page 71).

Makes 8.

VARIATIONS: Add ⅓ cup fruit, such as blueberries, chopped apples, chopped cranberries, or chopped bananas, or ¼ cup semisweet chocolate pieces, chopped nuts, grated coconut, or crumbled cooked bacon.

BISCUITS

Serve these light biscuits with any meal of the day, and try the variations. You can cut this biscuit dough into rounds or squares and bake them on top of chicken potpie.

3 cups Versatile Baking Mix
⅔ cup water

Preheat the oven to 450°F. Put the baking mix in a large bowl and make a well in the center. Pour in the water and mix quickly and lightly—about 25 strokes. Put the dough on a lightly floured surface and knead just until smooth—about 8 strokes. Pat or roll the dough to ½-inch thickness; cut with a 2½-inch round biscuit cutter, or cut into squares.
    Arrange biscuits in a well-greased 11" x 7" x 2" baking pan, barely touching each other. Bake 10 to 12 minutes, or until golden brown.

Makes about 12.

VARIATIONS: Add one or two of the following: ½ cup grated cheese; 1 tablespoon chopped fresh herbs; ¼ cup chopped, sautéed onions; ¼ cup crumbled cooked bacon or minced ham; or 1 tablespoon caraway, poppy, or sesame seeds.

CHEESE STICKS

These tasty bread sticks are great served with soup or chili.

1¹/₂ cups Versatile Baking Mix
¹/₂ cup grated sharp cheddar cheese
1 teaspoon poppy seeds
¹/₃ cup water

Preheat the oven to 450°F. In a medium bowl, toss the baking mix with the cheese and poppy seeds. Make a well and pour in the water. Mix lightly just until dry ingredients are moistened. Turn the dough onto a lightly floured board and knead 8 strokes. Pat or roll into a 12" x 8" rectangle. Cut into 12 1" x 8" strips. Roll the sticks between your palms and the floured surface to make ropes that are 12 inches long. Coat a baking sheet with nonstick spray coating, or grease lightly. Put the strips of dough on the baking sheet and bake about 10 minutes, or until light brown and crisp.

Makes 12.

COFFEECAKE

With a stock of Versatile Baking Mix (page 119) in your pantry, you can whip up a beautiful coffeecake in no time for breakfast or tea. You can make the streusel topping ahead of time, too, and refrigerate it for up to one month.

STREUSEL TOPPING
¹/₂ cup firmly packed brown sugar
¹/₂ teaspoon ground cinnamon
¹/₄ cup chopped nuts
2 tablespoons butter or margarine, softened

BATTER
2¹/₄ cups Versatile Baking Mix
¹/₄ cup granulated sugar or firmly packed brown sugar
¹/₃ cup water
1 egg
1 teaspoon vanilla

TO MAKE THE TOPPING: In a small bowl, toss together the sugar, cinnamon, and nuts. With a fork, blend in the butter or margarine until mixture is crumbly. Set aside.

TO MAKE THE BATTER: Preheat the oven to 375°F. In a medium bowl, toss together the baking mix and sugar; add the water, egg, and vanilla. Mix until well blended. Spread into a greased 8" x 8" baking pan. Sprinkle the streusel topping evenly over the batter. Bake about 20 minutes, or until a toothpick inserted in the center comes out clean. Cut into squares and serve warm.

Makes 6 servings.

VARIATION: Add 1¹/₂ teaspoons finely shredded fresh orange or lemon peel to the batter or, for the holidays, add 2 tablespoons chopped candied citron or candied lemon peel.

■ *Cheese Sticks (left); Coffeecake (below)*

JAMAICAN-STYLE MEAT TRIANGLES

For a quick dinner, make the spicy filling and pastry dough for these meat-filled triangles early in the day or the night before and refrigerate them separately, then form and bake the triangles. Serve with Apple-Peach-Raisin Chutney (page 89) or Mom's Bread-and-Butter Pickles (page 85), corn, and coleslaw.

FILLING
¼ pound lean ground beef or raw chicken
1 green onion, minced (including green part)
¼ cup chopped green bell pepper
2 tablespoons chopped red bell pepper
1 teaspoon Garam Masala (page 110), Arizona Chili Powder (page 112), or curry powder
1 teaspoon all-purpose flour
¼ teaspoon salt

PASTRY DOUGH
2 cups Versatile Baking Mix
¼ teaspoon ground turmeric (for yellow color; optional)
½ cup dairy sour cream or plain yogurt
1 egg

GLAZE
1 egg yolk beaten with 1 tablespoon water

To make the filling: In a large nonstick skillet, cook the beef or chicken, green onions, peppers, and Garam Masala, chili powder, or curry powder until the beef is brown and the vegetables are tender; drain if necessary. Stir in flour and salt. Set aside to cool.

To make the pastry dough: Preheat the oven to 375°F. In a medium bowl, stir together the baking mix and turmeric, if

using. Stir in the sour cream or yogurt and egg until dough is thick and smooth. Shape into a round and flatten slightly; wrap and refrigerate for at least 1 hour or up to 24 hours. Divide the dough in half and roll half the pastry dough to a 12-inch square on a generously floured surface. Cut into 4 6-inch squares. Repeat with the second half for a total of 8 squares.

Mound a rounded tablespoon of filling in the center of each square. Brush the edges of the dough with water. Fold a corner of the dough over the filling to form a triangle. Press with a fork to seal. Prick the top with a fork.

Brush the glaze on the triangles. On a lightly greased baking sheet, bake 25 to 30 minutes, or until golden brown.

Makes 8 large triangles.

VARIATIONS: For hors d'oeuvres, cut pastry into 24 3-inch rounds. Place 1 teaspoon filling in the center of each round. Brush the edges of the dough with water. Fold into a half-moon shape. Refrigerate them, unbaked, for up to 24 hours. You can bake the hors d'oeuvres in a 375°F oven for 25 to 30 minutes, then serve. Or, cool and freeze the baked hors d'oeuvres, well-wrapped, until party time (up to 3 months). To serve, thaw and pop in the oven for 15 minutes to heat. Makes 24.

For meatless triangles, omit the ground beef or chicken. In a small saucepan, cook the green onions, peppers, and seasonings, covered, in 2 tablespoons water for about 5 minutes, or until tender. Stir in the flour and salt. Stir in ½ cup mashed cooked kidney, pinto, or garbanzo beans and ½ cup canned or cooked and drained whole kernel corn.

WHOLE-WHEAT CORNBREAD MIX

This convenient mix is just bursting with grainy goodness. Combining a corn product and beans and/or milk creates a complete protein, so mix up cornbread or muffins to serve with black-eyed peas, lentil soup, chili, macaroni and cheese, baked beans, or vegetable stews or curries.

10 cups (2½ pounds) whole-wheat flour
5 cups (1⅔ pounds) cornmeal
½ cup sugar
⅓ cup baking powder
2 tablespoons salt
1½ teaspoons cream of tartar
3 cups (1½ pounds) shortening (that does not require refrigeration)

In a very large bowl, stir together the flour, cornmeal, sugar, baking powder, salt, and cream of tartar. With a pastry blender, cut the shortening into the flour mixture thoroughly until it resembles coarse sand. Store in tightly covered glass or plastic containers or self-sealing bags for up to 6 weeks at room temperature or for up to 6 months in the freezer. To use, pile the mix lightly in a measuring cup and level with a spatula or knife.

Makes about 15 cups.

- *Double-Corn Cornbread made with Whole-Wheat Cornbread Mix*

Recipes for using Whole-Wheat Cornbread Mix:

DOUBLE-CORN CORNBREAD OR MUFFINS

Moist and light, this cornbread is great served hot with butter. Or enjoy it as my late friend Johnnie Lee Macfadden did—crumble cornbread or muffins into a tall glass, cover with milk and a little sugar, and eat it with a spoon.

4 teaspoons shortening (for cornbread only)
2 1/2 cups Whole-Wheat Cornbread Mix
1 can (8 3/4 ounces) cream-style corn
3/4 cup milk
1 egg

Preheat the oven to 400°F.

FOR CORNBREAD: Put shortening in a 9" x 9" baking pan or a 9" round cast-iron skillet and heat in the oven until melted and the skillet is hot. Meanwhile, put bread mix in a medium bowl. In a small bowl, thoroughly mix together the corn, milk, and egg. Pour the corn/milk mixture into the dry mix and stir lightly, just until the mix is moistened. Lift and tilt to spread hot shortening in pan. Pour batter into the hot pan—this will give the cornbread a brown crispy crust. Bake 20 to 25 minutes, or until golden brown and a toothpick inserted in the center comes out clean.

FOR MUFFINS: Grease 15 2 1/2-inch muffin cups or coat with nonstick spray coating. Mix the cornbread batter as described at left, omitting the hot shortening, and spoon the batter evenly into the muffin cups, filling each two-thirds full. Bake 20 minutes, or until golden. Remove from muffin cups while hot and serve from a napkin-lined basket.

Makes 9 servings of cornbread or 15 muffins.

VARIATIONS: Add one of the following: 1/4 cup chopped green or red bell peppers and/or 1 tablespoon grated onions with corn mixture; 1 teaspoon chili powder and/or 1/2 cup shredded cheese; 2 tablespoons sugar and 1 cup fresh or frozen blueberries; or top muffins with 1 teaspoon Red and Green Bell Pepper Jelly (page 74) before baking.

CORN WAFFLES

Serve these grainy golden waffles for brunch, topped with whipped cream cheese or butter and Strawberry Freezer Jam (page 71), Preserved Lemony Figs (page 77), or Brandied Jam Sauce (page 100). Or, have them for dinner with creamed chicken, mushrooms, or spicy chili. Freeze leftover waffles and reheat in a toaster.

2 1/4 cups Whole-Wheat Cornbread Mix
1 1/2 cups milk
2 eggs
1/4 cup melted butter, shortening, or bacon drippings

Grease waffle iron, if necessary, and heat. Put bread mix in a medium bowl. In a small bowl, stir together the milk, eggs, and butter, shortening, or bacon drippings. Pour the milk mixture into the dry mix and stir lightly, just until the mix is moistened. Pour batter into waffle iron, covering about two-thirds of the surface. Bake about 4 minutes, or until steam stops escaping from the sides or indicator light goes off.

Makes 12 4-inch waffles.

EMPTY MUFFIN CUPS

If you've used all the batter for muffins or cupcakes and you have empty muffin cups in the tin, fill those empty cups to two-thirds full with water. If you've already greased the cups, the water prevents the grease from burning onto the cup.

▪ *Corn Waffles made with Whole-Wheat Cornbread Mix*

■ *Cornbread-Topped Chili made with Whole-Wheat Cornbread Mix*

CORNBREAD-TOPPED CHILI

The chili in this recipe is thin before you bake it; the cornbread topping absorbs much of the liquid, leaving a nice thick chili underneath.

CHILI

1 pound ground beef or raw chicken
1 large onion, chopped
2 cloves garlic, minced
1 teaspoon to 2 tablespoons Arizona Chili Powder (page 112) or commercial chili powder
1 can (16 ounces) crushed or diced tomatoes
1/2 cup water or red wine
2 cans (16 ounces each) red kidney and/or pinto beans, drained and rinsed
1 teaspoon sugar
3/4 teaspoon salt
1/2 teaspoon hot-pepper sauce (optional)

TOPPING

2 cups Whole-Wheat Cornbread Mix
3/4 cup milk
1 egg, lightly beaten

TO MAKE THE CHILI: Preheat the oven to 375°F. In a 12-inch nonstick skillet, cook the ground beef or chicken with the onions and garlic until the meat is brown and the onion is tender. Drain any fat. Stir in the chili powder; cook 1 minute more. Stir in the tomatoes (with juice), water or wine, beans, sugar, salt, and hot-pepper sauce. Bring to a boil, reduce heat, and simmer, covered, for 15 minutes. Pour hot chili into a 3-quart rectangular baking dish.

TO MAKE THE TOPPING: In a medium bowl, stir together the bread mix, milk, and egg just until dry ingredients are moistened. Drop the batter in 1/4-cup portions on the hot chili. Bake 20 minutes, or until the cornbread is golden brown and the chili is bubbling. For a special meal, serve with salsa, shredded cheese, dairy sour cream, chopped raw onions, and/or chopped avocados.

Makes 4 to 6 servings.

VARIATION: For meatless chili, omit the beef or chicken and add an additional 16-ounce can of kidney of pinto beans.

CORN STICKS

A cast-iron corn stick mold is needed to make this recipe. For a thoughtful holiday gift, wrap up a corn stick mold and a canister of Whole-Wheat Cornbread Mix. When not in use, the mold looks nice hanging on the wall of a country kitchen.

About 1 1/2 tablespoons shortening
2 cups Whole-Wheat Cornbread Mix
1 cup milk
1 egg
2 tablespoons melted butter or shortening

Preheat the oven to 425°F. Put a scant 1/4 teaspoon shortening in each of 15 cast-iron corn stick molds. Put the molds in the oven until the shortening is melted and the molds are hot. Meanwhile, put the bread mix in a medium bowl. In a small bowl, stir together the milk, egg, and melted butter or shortening. Pour the milk mixture into the dry mix and stir lightly, just until the mix is moistened. Put batter into hot corn stick molds—no more than half full—and bake 15 minutes, or until golden brown.

Makes 15.

EIGHT-BEAN SOUP MIX

One Christmas, in a gift catalog, I saw a bean mix similar to this—the colorful beans layered in a bean-pot-shaped glass jar tied with a huge gold and brown ribbon and a $40 price tag! Make the mix at a fraction of that cost and remember: Presentation is everything.

1 cup dry pinto or red kidney beans
1 cup dry black beans
1 cup dry yellow split peas
1 cup dry black-eyed peas
1 cup dry red or brown lentils
1 cup dry green split peas
1 cup dry navy beans
1 cup dry adzuki beans

Line up 4 or 5 clean pint jars; spoon about 2 tablespoons pinto or kidney beans evenly in the bottom of each jar. Continue adding about 2 tablespoons of each bean in the order given until the jars are full. Cover the jars and store for up to 1 year at room temperature.

Makes 4 or 5 pint jars.

■ *Eight-Bean Soup Mix*

TO MAKE SOUP WITH EIGHT-BEAN SOUP MIX:

1 pint Eight-Bean Soup Mix
14 cups water, divided
1 large onion, chopped
2 carrots, peeled and chopped
1 rib celery, chopped (including leaves)
1 can (15 ounces) tomato sauce
1 tablespoon ground cumin
1 to 2 teaspoons salt
1 tablespoon fresh lemon juice

Rinse the beans and discard those that are very wrinkled or that float. Put the beans in a large pot (at least 4 quarts). Cover the beans with 7 cups of the water. Bring to a boil, then reduce the heat. Simmer for 2 minutes. Cover, remove from the heat, and let stand 1 hour. Drain, rinse in a colander, and add 7 cups fresh water.

Add the onions, carrots, celery, tomato sauce, cumin, and salt. Bring to a boil, lower the heat, and simmer, covered, for 1½ to 2 hours, or until the beans are tender. Stir in the lemon juice.

Makes 6 to 8 servings.

VARIATION: If you include bags of Herb Mix for Soup or Stock (page 112) as a gift, directions for making Eight-Bean Soup should include omitting the cumin and adding 2 bags of herb mix (with a sprig of fresh parsley tied to each bag) after the soup has cooked for 30 minutes.

OATMEAL COOKIE MIX

My sister, Gail Berry, made a batch of this mix, put it in tall cork-topped glass canisters, tied plaid bows around them, labeled them with baking instructions, and gave them as Christmas gifts. Everybody loves these cookies! They're soft and chewy, delicious, and nutritious.

3 cups all-purpose flour
1½ cups granulated sugar
1½ cups firmly packed brown sugar
1 tablespoon baking powder
1 teaspoon salt
½ teaspoon baking soda
2 cups vegetable shortening (that does not require refrigeration)
6 cups regular or quick-cooking rolled oats

In a very large bowl, combine the flour, sugar, brown sugar, baking powder, salt, and baking soda. With a pastry blender, cut in the shortening until the mixture resembles small peas. Stir in the oats. Divide the mixture into 4 portions, about 4 cups in each. Store in self-sealing freezer bags up to 6 months in the freezer.

Makes 16 cups mix; enough for 12 dozen cookies.

TO MAKE COOKIES WITH OATMEAL COOKIE MIX:

One portion Oatmeal Cookie Mix
2 eggs
2 teaspoons vanilla

Preheat the oven to 350°F. In a large bowl, combine all the ingredients until moistened. (The mixture will seem too dry at first, but keep stirring.) Drop the dough by teaspoonfuls onto a lightly greased cookie sheet (flatten with a fork if desired) and bake 10 to 12 minutes, or until the edges are light brown. Cool on wire racks.

Makes 3 dozen cookies.

VARIATIONS: Stir one of the following into the mix before adding eggs and vanilla: 1 package (6 ounces) semisweet or milk chocolate, peanut butter, or butterscotch pieces; 3/4 cup raisins; 1 cup chopped nuts; or 1 teaspoon ground cinnamon.

HOT COCOA MIX

Hot cocoa, so warm and comforting, can be made in an instant with this inexpensive mix. For a last-minute gift, put a batch of this mix (1 2/3 cups) in a plastic self-sealing bag, and put the bag and directions for making the beverage in a mug with a ribbon tied to the handle.

2 3/4 cups nonfat dry milk powder
1 1/2 cups presweetened cocoa powder
1/2 cup powdered nondairy creamer
1/2 cup powdered sugar
Dash of salt
1 cup tiny marshmallows (optional)

In a medium bowl, stir all the ingredients together until combined. Pour into a plastic container or glass jar, cover, and keep at room temperature for up to 6 months.

Makes 5 cups mix; enough for 15 servings.

VARIATIONS: For almond-, Irish cream-, or vanilla-flavored mix, use 1 cup presweetened cocoa powder and 1 cup powdered flavored nondairy creamer in the flavor of your choice. Omit the 1/2 cup nondairy creamer and the 1/2 cup powdered sugar.

For mocha-flavored mix, add 2 tablespoons instant regular or decaffeinated coffee crystals.

TO MAKE BEVERAGE: Put 1/3 cup cocoa mix in a mug with 3/4 cup boiling water and stir until smooth.

VARIATION: For iced cocoa: Make beverage with hot (not boiling) water. Fill a tall glass with ice cubes and pour the beverage over the ice. Top with whipped cream and a dash of cinnamon, if you like.

CITRUS TEA MIX

This sugar-free mix can be used to make a hot or cold beverage.

1 cup lemon-flavored iced tea mix sweetened with non-nutritive sweetener
3 tablespoons orange-flavored instant breakfast drink powder sweetened with non-nutritive sweetener
1 package (0.46 ounce) sugar-free lemonade drink mix

Mix all ingredients in a bowl and store in a covered plastic or glass container at room temperature for up to 6 months. Stir again before using.

Makes scant 1 1/4 cups; enough for 40 hot servings or 20 iced servings.

TO MAKE HOT BEVERAGE: Put 3/4 cup boiling water in a tea cup and add 1 1/2 teaspoons tea mix; stir well.

TO MAKE ICED BEVERAGE: Fill a tall glass with ice cubes and add 1 tablespoon mix. Fill with water and stir well.

▪ *Cookies made with Oatmeal Cookie Mix; Hot Cocoa made with Hot Cocoa Mix*

CHAPTER 6

Sweet Treats

AS IT GETS CLOSER TO THE HOLI-
DAYS, YOU WILL NO DOUBT FILL
YOUR HOME WITH THE HEAVENLY
SMELL OF BAKING COOKIES. HOW-
EVER, HERE ARE A FEW THINGS
YOU CAN MAKE NOW AND KEEP,

THEN PULL OUT AS A FORGOTTEN
SURPRISE WHEN THE HOLIDAYS
ARRIVE. THEY WILL ALSO BE
TERRIFIC BREAD-AND-BUTTER
GIFTS FOR THE MANY PARTIES
DURING THE CHRISTMAS SEASON.

■ *Holiday Fruit 'n' Nut Balls*

Candies

Here are recipes for candies you can make now that will store well and even improve with time. They're great to have on hand—you can take a box of homemade candy as a hostess gift or send a box to your child's teacher.

HOLIDAY FRUIT 'N' NUT BALLS

These candy balls have a fruitcakelike consistency and a sweet/tart flavor from dried fruits. Serve them on a dessert tray or put them in small paper baking cups and box for gift-giving. These candies mail well. This recipe makes a lot of candy. If you would like to make less, halve all the ingredients except use ½ cup evaporated milk.

1 pound graham crackers
8 cups mixed unsalted nuts (almonds, pecans, walnuts, brazil nuts, and/or hazel nuts), coarsely chopped
2 cups golden raisins
2 cups dark raisins
2 cups dried apricots, coarsely chopped
2 cups dates, coarsely chopped
1 pound marshmallows
¾ cup evaporated milk
2 cups grated coconut (optional)

Break up the graham crackers, put in a blender or food processor fitted with a metal blade, and whirl, about one-third at a time, until the crackers are crushed to fine crumbs. Put the crumbs, nuts, raisins, apricots, and dates in a large bowl and mix them together. In a pan over medium heat, melt the marshmallows in the milk, stirring constantly. Pour the hot marshmallow mixture over the crumb mixture. Mix thoroughly.

Cover several baking sheets with plastic wrap. Form the mixture into lumpy balls by rounded tablespoons. Roll the balls in coconut, if using. Place the balls on the baking sheets and freeze for 1 hour. Remove frozen balls to self-sealing freezer bags or plastic containers. Freeze for up to 4 months. Thaw overnight in the refrigerator before serving.

Makes about 12 dozen.

CRACKLING PEANUT BRITTLE

This brittle is so thin, it crackles. The secret is to pull the candy while it's hot—use two forks. If you mail this candy, insulate it well so it doesn't arrive in a million tiny shards.

2 cups sugar
1 cup light corn syrup
1 cup water
2 cups raw peanuts (small Spanish peanuts are best)
¼ cup butter
1 teaspoon vanilla
1½ teaspoons baking soda

Butter the sides of a heavy 3-quart saucepan. Combine sugar, corn syrup, and water in the saucepan. Cook over medium-high heat, stirring constantly, until boiling. Clip candy thermometer to the side of the pan. Cook over medium-low heat for 25 to 30 minutes, or until the candy thermometer registers 275°F or until a small amount dropped into

cold water separates into threads that bend when removed from the water. Butter a very large baking sheet. Add the peanuts to the sugar mixture and continue cooking for 10 to 15 minutes, or until the candy thermometer registers 295°F or until a small amount dropped into cold water separates into threads that crack when removed from the water. Remove from the heat and remove the thermometer. Stir in the butter and vanilla. Quickly sprinkle the baking soda over the mixture, stirring constantly. Quickly pour the candy out onto the baking sheet. Stretch the candy by using two forks to lift and pull the candy as it cools. Cool thoroughly and break into pieces. Store in a covered tin or plastic container at room temperature for up to 3 months.

Makes about 2 pounds.

VARIATION: Substitute raw cashews or whole raw almonds; or use a combination of two or more kinds of nuts instead of the peanuts.

▪ *Crackling Peanut Brittle (top) and Creamy Brown Candy (bottom)*

CREAMY BROWN CANDY

Not really fudge and not exactly taffy, this candy is in a category by itself. And, it stays moist and creamy almost indefinitely in the refrigerator—if you hide it away! You can mail Creamy Brown Candy in cold weather.

3 cups sugar, divided
1 cup half-and-half or light cream
¼ teaspoon baking soda
¼ cup butter
⅛ teaspoon salt
1 teaspoon vanilla
½ cup chopped pecans

Butter an 8" x 8" baking pan. Mix 2 cups of the sugar with the cream in a heavy 2-quart saucepan over low heat. In a small heavy skillet, heat the remaining 1 cup sugar over medium-high heat, without stirring, until the sugar begins to melt. Shake the skillet occasionally. Reduce the heat to low and cook, stirring frequently, until the sugar is golden brown and completely melted. Slowly stir into sugar/cream mixture. Cook and stir over low heat until mixture registers 244°F on a candy thermometer or until a small amount forms a firm ball when dropped in cold water. Remove from the heat. Stir in the baking soda and stir vigorously. Add the butter and salt and let stand without stirring for 20 minutes. Add the vanilla. Beat with a wooden spoon until the candy is thick and has a dull appearance. Add the nuts and turn into the prepared pan. With buttered hands, press the mixture to the edges of the pan. Cut into small squares. Refrigerate, well-covered, for up to 2 weeks or freeze for up to 6 months.

Makes 1½ pounds.

Cordials and Liqueurs

Poured into tall decanters, homemade cordials are enchanting hostess gifts during the holiday season. Quick to make, the flavors of cordials intensify and improve as the drinks sit on a shelf for weeks. When the flavors have fully developed, just paste on a label and decorate the fancy bottles with ribbons.

The terms cordial and liqueur are interchangeable—both meaning a sweet, flavored alcoholic beverage. For best results, use only the finest ingredients, including a good-quality vodka.

CRANBERRY CORDIAL

A sweet, rosy-colored after-dinner drink, Cranberry Cordial can be sprinkled on pound cake, then topped with layers of raspberries and vanilla pudding for a tipsy holiday trifle. Make a batch of this beverage as soon as fresh cranberries come to market and the cordial will be ready by Thanksgiving.

4 cups fresh cranberries
2½ cups sugar
1 tablespoon finely shredded orange peel
4 whole cloves
1 cinnamon stick (4 inches), broken in half
4 cups vodka

Rinse the cranberries and pick out any that are shriveled. Chop the cranberries coarsely with a knife or in a food processor. In a large bowl, mix together the cranberries, sugar, and orange peel. Divide the mixture into 2 clean quart-size glass jars. Add 2 cloves and half the cinnamon stick to each jar. Stir half the vodka into each jar. Cover the jars tightly and store in a cool place for 1 month, shaking at least once a week.

Strain the mixture into a large bowl through a sieve lined with two layers of 100% cotton cheesecloth. Twist the cheesecloth tightly until the cranberries are as dry as possible. Discard cranberries. Pour the cordial into decorative bottles and cap or cork (with new corks) tightly. Keeps indefinitely.

Makes about 2 pints.

ACAPULCO COFFEE LIQUEUR

You and your guests will enjoy the deep coffee flavor of this liqueur. For a welcome winter warmer, pour a finger of Acapulco Coffee Liqueur into hot coffee and top it with a dollop of whipped cream and a sprinkle of cinnamon. Or, serve over cracked ice.

5 cups sugar
1 jar (2 ounces) instant coffee
4 cups boiling water
4 cups vodka
1 vanilla bean, cut into 3 pieces

In a large bowl, mix together the sugar and coffee. Pour the water into the mixture and stir; cover and let cool to room temperature. Stir in the vodka. Pour into 3 clean quart-size glass jars. Drop a piece of vanilla bean into each jar. Cover tightly and store in a dark place for 2 weeks, shaking at least once a week. Remove and discard the vanilla beans and transfer the liqueur into decorative bottles; cap or cork (with new corks) tightly. Keeps indefinitely.

Makes about 4½ pints.

PEPPERMINT APERITIF

A little bit of mint goes a long way in this flavored liqueur. Serve it in small glasses with coffee after dessert. Or, you may like to add an ounce of Peppermint Aperitif to a cup of strong, hot coffee and finish with whipped cream and a red and white peppermint stick. It is also great poured over vanilla ice cream.

3 cups sugar
3 cups water
¾ cup chopped fresh peppermint or spearmint leaves
3 cups vodka
A few drops green food coloring (optional)

Make a simple syrup by simmering the sugar and water together in a large saucepan just until the sugar is dissolved; let cool. Put half of the mint leaves in each of 2 clean quart-size glass jars. Equally divide the syrup and vodka between the jars. Cover tightly and store in a cool place for 1 week. Taste the liqueur; if you want a more powerful mint flavor, store for 1 week more.

Strain the liqueur into a large bowl through a sieve lined with two layers of 100% cotton cheesecloth. Discard the mint. Add drops of green food coloring, if using, until the desired color is achieved. Pour the liqueur into decorative bottles and cap or cork (with new corks) tightly. Keeps indefinitely.

Makes about 3½ pints.

▪ *Cranberry Cordial; Acapulco Coffee Liqueur*

SEALING WITH STYLE

You can give your gift bottles of cordials or herb vinegars a very special and stylish look by sealing them with ribbon and wax.

First, seal the bottle with a capper (you need special equipment for this) or a new cork. Then, melt wax (paraffin, candle ends, or crayons) in an old metal can placed in a pan of simmering water. Be very careful to keep the wax away from the flame, because it is flammable.

Choose a satin or grosgrain ribbon that is narrower than the bottle top is wide. Cut a length of ribbon that will go across the top of the bottle and down two sides at least three inches on each side (about seven inches in all).

Hold the ribbon securely over the bottle top and carefully dip the top of the sealed bottle into the hot wax. Let the wax cool and harden. If the wax is thin, you may have to dip it several times to get a thick layer of wax.

To open the bottle, simply pull up one end of the ribbon to break the wax seal.

SOURCES

Most of the supplies called for in the directions for the projects in this book are available in craft stores. If you have difficulty finding specific items, contact the manufacturer for a listing of suppliers in your area.

TRAY FOR FLOWERS, BUTTERFLY, AND RIBBON TRAY AVAILABLE THROUGH:
Sudberry House
Box 895
Old Lyme, CT 06371
(800) 243-2607

BOX FOR FATHER CHRISTMAS SHADOW BOX AVAILABLE THROUGH:
Mueller-Wood Kraft, Inc.
233425 W. Wall Street
Lake Villa, IL 60046
(708) 395-0005

SLEIGH FOR FRUITFUL SLEIGH AVAILABLE THROUGH:
The Wooden Hen
73389 SR 45
Lisbon, OH 44432
(216) 424-0088

ACCENT PAINTS
300 East Main Street
Lake Zurich, IL 60047
(708) 540-1604

COATS & CLARK/ANCHOR (EMBROIDERY FLOSS)
Consumer Service Dept.
30 Patewood Drive
Greenville, SC 29615
(800) 648-1479

DMC CORPORATION (EMBROIDERY FLOSS)
Port Kearny Building #10
South Kearny, NJ 07032
(201) 589-0606

FREUDENBERG NONWOVENS (PELLON)
20 Industrial Avenue
Chelmsford, MA 01824
(508) 454-0461

KREINIK MANUFACTURING CO. (METALLIC THREAD)
P.O. Box 1966
Parkersburg, WV 26102
(304) 422-8900

C.M. OFFRAY AND SON (RIBBONS)
Route 24
Chester, NJ 07930
(908) 879-4700

ROBERT SIMMONS, INC. (ARTISTS' BRUSHES)
45 West 18th Street
New York, NY 10011
(212) 675-3136

VELCRO USA, INC.
P.O. Box 5218
406 Brown Avenue
Manchester, NH 03108
(603) 669-4892

ZWEIGART (NEEDLEWORK FABRICS)
Weston Canal Plaza
2 Riverview Drive
Somerset, NJ 08873
(908) 271-1949

DESIGNERS

Our special thanks to the following designers who contributed projects for this book:

YVONNE BEECHER—Home and Hearts Sampler, page 16; Reindeer Tree Skirt, page 46; Tartan Desk Set, page 58

MARINA GRANT—Fruitful Sleigh, page 52

SHARON HOYER—Snowflake Afghan, page 26

ROSEMARY SANDBERG-PADDEN—Holly Heart Stocking, page 43

GINGER HANSEN SHAFER—Golden Ribbon Pillows, page 23; Richly Ribboned Stocking, page 39; Celestial Boot, page 44; Father Christmas Shadow Box, page 48; Family Photo Frames, page 62

MIMI SHIMMIN—Victorian Shapes, page 31; Ribbon Embroidered Geometrics, page 33; Christmas Star Stocking, page 39; Folk Art Christmas Stocking, page 41

JACKIE SMYTH—Pine Tree Quilt, page 21; Potpourri Ornaments, page 35

BARBARA SWANSON—Flowers, Bows, and Butterflies Dresser Tray, page 56

PROP CREDITS

WE ARE GRATEFUL TO THE FOLLOWING COMPANIES FOR THE LOAN OF MANY FINE ITEMS FOR USE IN THE PHOTOGRAPHY. THOSE ITEMS NOT INDIVIDUALLY LISTED WE OBTAINED PRIVATELY.

CRAFT PROPS:
Page 16: topiary—The Garden Shop, Glen Ridge, NJ; Page 20: swag, embroidered pillows, and basket—Midwest Importers of Cannon Falls, MN; plate—Hartstone, Zanesville, OH; Page 46: Christmas tree—All Western Evergreen Nursery, Webster's Crossing, NY; ribbons—C.M. Offray and Son, Chester, NJ; tree topper—Midwest Importers of Cannon Falls, MN; Page 48: wooden Santas—Midwestern Importers of Cannon Falls, MN; Page 52: ornaments—Old World Christmas, Spokane, WA; plates—Lorraine Tully Antiques and Decorative Accessories, Upper Montclair, NJ; Page 55: ornaments—Old World Christmas, Spokane, WA; ribbons—C.M. Offray and Son, Chester, NJ; Page 61: lamp, pen, letter opener, and magnifying glass—Bombay Company, Fort Worth, TX; Page 62: topiary—The Garden Shop, Glen Ridge, NJ.

FOOD PROPS:
Pages 64 & 76: plate—Pottery Barn, New York, NY; mug, teapot, cream & sugar—William-Wayne & Company, New York, NY; Page 70: jam jar—William-Wayne & Company, New York, NY; Page 74: wicker tray & glasses—William-Wayne & Company, New York, NY; napkin & fork—Pottery Barn, New York, NY; Page 91: 3 vases, water glass—Zona, New York, NY; Page 96: Page 94: teapot, trivet, cup & saucer, flatware, egg basket—Zona, New York, NY; Page 96: stemmed glass—Union Street Glass, Oakland, CA; plate—Cyclamen Studio, Berkeley, CA; glass dish—Zona, New York, NY; Page 97: teapot & basket—William-Wayne & Company, New York, NY; Page 101: ice cream dishes—Pottery Barn, New York, NY; Page 104: plate—Fioreware, Zanesville, OH; Page 105: flatware—Pottery Barn, New York, NY; plate—Cyclamen Studio, Berkeley, CA; Page 115: tray—Zona, New York, NY; Page 121: Barn, New York, NY; Page 118: plate, teapot, vase—Pottery Barn, New York, NY; glass mugs—Pottery coffee set—Cuthbertson Imports Inc., Norwalk, CT; Page 123: 3 bowls—Zona, New York, NY; Page 125: napkin, flatware—Pottery Barn, New York, NY; plate—Cyclamen Studio, Berkeley, CA; cup & saucer—Zona, New York, NY; Page 126: soup bowl—Pottery Barn, New York, NY; Page 131: cup & plate—Cuthbertson Imports Inc., Norwalk, CT; Page 136: cordial glasses—Union Street Glass, Oakland, CA; tiered candy dish—Cuthbertson Imports Inc., Norwalk, CT; tray—Zona, New York, NY; Page 139: tray & cordial glasses—Cuthbertson Imports Inc., Norwalk, CT.

INDEX